The education officer
and his world

The education officer and his world

Derek Birley

London
Routledge and Kegan Paul

First published in 1970
by Routledge and Kegan Paul Limited,
Broadway House, 68-74 Carter Lane,
London E.C.4
Printed in Great Britain
by Clarke, Doble & Brendon Limited, Plymouth
© Derek Birley, 1970
ISBN 0 7100 6811 5

Contents

Acknowledgements

Many people have helped with this book, either consciously or unconsciously. I cannot name each one individually, but I should like to thank them most sincerely. The mistakes are, of course, my own.

One person must be mentioned. I have depended heavily upon Mrs. Marjorie Gillespie during office hours for a long time. Now she has put me even further in her debt by spending her spare time typing, with great skill and good humour, innumerable drafts of a long manuscript.

Introduction

Of the millions of words written on British education remarkably few have been about its administration. In spite of its elaborately democratic framework the people for whom the education service is intended, and who pay for it, tend to know little of the way it works. Even teachers may have a hazy idea of what goes on behind the scenes in their own Authority. If they harbour dark suspicions this is hardly surprising for the activities of educational administrators are less well documented than those of MI5.

There is no shortage of historical or descriptive surveys of the education system or treatises on legal aspects, statistics and economic issues. What is missing is analysis of the administrative process itself : anyone thinking of taking up a career in administration is likely to be disappointed if he looks for a book that will give him some idea of what may be expected of him.

This applies to the public services generally, not just education. Whatever the promise of their titles books on administration tend to concern themselves with the surface not the heart of the matter. Such analysis as there is appears to have been carried out by practically everybody except administrators. There are journalistic assessments, political revaluations, nostalgic yearnings for the simple life, comical caricatures and academic theories of reform; but few attempts by administrators to write about the philosophical basis of their craft, outline their techniques, examine the practical problems they encounter or suggest new methods of approach. The result is not merely widespread public misunderstanding about the activities and motivation of administrators but too little inter-change of ideas amongst the professionals themselves.

Whatever its other merits, then, this book should have a certain rarity value. It is about administration itself, not some incidental aspect of it, and it was written by a practising administrator. It concerns educational administration where there is not so much a gap to be filled as a ghastly void. Its first aim is simply to shed light on a darkish place, but beyond that it tries to make a contribution to constructive discussion of a problem that confronts all administrators and particularly those in the education service.

Everyone agrees on the need to transform the public services and to bring modern techniques into the processes of government. The argument is about how it should be done. Education officers feel themselves especially threatened by the assumption that management experts knowing nothing of education can nevertheless take their service by the scruff of the neck and shake it into efficiency. They are reluctant to accept that the doctrine 'he who is trained in management can administer anything' applies to education. Unfortunately the undoubted strength of the case against an extremist application of this doctrine is weakened when educationists who feel threatened retreat into shell-backed resistance to change, or give the impression that they wish to spend their days thinking beautiful thoughts about education or patting children on the head.

There is at present a chasm between those who see education as a business to be managed and those who see it as a garden full of delicate plants. This book is an expression of a personal conviction about the way to bridge the gap: to regard the opposing elements not as sources of division but as keys to understanding the nature of the service. If the tension can be resolved in this way educational administration ceases to be an uneasy confrontation of business methods and esoteric philosophy, and becomes a unique and integrated complex of techniques in its own right.

There are other tensions for the education officer. Education must be highly sensitive to local needs, yet it must be a national service without regional anomalies; it must provide equal opportunities for all, yet it must not neglect those with special needs; it must be democratically-based, yet it must be planned and efficiently and economically run. Those now engaged in educational administration seem to have the hardest job of any in the public service. If this is true, then it is an excellent reason for a detailed examination of what they do. If it is not, but merely that they make it look difficult, perhaps there is an even greater need for investigation.

'Educational administration' is currently used to describe anything from preparing a school time-table to running a branch of the Department of Education and Science. Concentrating here on the work of full-time professional education officers of local authorities is not intended as a comment on this usage : it arises mainly from the need to set some bounds to an otherwise amorphous task. However, it does seem that this side of educational administration is the one in which the contemporary dilemma is at its most acute. Furthermore it is the most neglected part of generally neglected territory.

That education officers themselves have written practically nothing on the subject is curious, particularly as the teaching profession from which almost all senior educational administrators are drawn is so articulate. It is not for want of thought or concern; nor is it because they do not recognize their dilemma. British traditions are of course based on high esteem for skilful practice rather than on theories, and there are clear dangers that too much theorizing by the practitioners might lead to an unhelpful self-consciousness in the personal relationships that are at the heart of good administration.

On the other hand the recent (and very necessary) application of management thinking to public service problems can quickly lead to a situation in which everybody has something to say about how to manage education except those who do the job at the moment. And that would be ridiculous. This book stems from the conviction first that education officers have something of value to contribute about the needs and problems of management in education, and second that if they do not come to grips with the changing needs of their service they must expect to make room for a different breed of men.

No one is likely to imagine that this sketch of the battlefield is intended as a master-plan for winning the war. It is an attempt to look at the scene from one particular angle : others may see it differently. If it provokes discussion this may help to draw attention to some of the urgent problems facing a great and growing service in which everyone has a stake.

1

The nature
of educational
administration

Becoming an administrator is not the only way of incurring odium, but it is as effective as most. This is hardly surprising. For one thing administration is not complete in itself, like house-building or all-in wrestling: it is merely a means of implementing policy. So at its best it is unobtrusive and can therefore be taken for granted. It becomes noticeable only when it is badly done or when it seeks to implement unpopular policies.

Why then should anyone want to become an administrator? Is it a disreputable desire to manipulate and manage; or an altruistic wish to serve the public? Is it an unheroic urge to seek refuge in a backroom; or an aspect of social concern? Is it interest in the work itself or in the security and respectability it brings? You can find all these and a dozen more motives by peering past the filing cabinets and tea-cups into any public office.

It is no easier to generalize about administrators than it is about builders or wrestlers. And if one common characteristic is singled out amongst all the other, various ones, even that can look different according to the point of view. Perhaps the perspective of history will show the spread of administration in our time as no more than parasitic growth, an aspect of decadence. From the inside and from the perspective of today, though, there seems to be another explanation. As life grows more complex and government enters into personal affairs increasingly and in more subtle ways so the need increases for those who feel concern about the way society develops to try to make the processes of government work better.

The origin of the species

The explanation seems to fit educational administration. Almost all senior education officers were originally teachers, which argues a degree of social concern, and it is difficult to explain why they subsequently forsake the schools and colleges except in terms of a desire to improve the service at the point where policies are decided and begin to be implemented. What other reasons are there?

Fame and glory can certainly be discounted: perhaps the best known education officer owed his celebrity to performing on the wireless in another context altogether. Popularity and affection can be better acquired in almost any other sphere. Some would tell you that masochism was nearer the mark but this is probably intended as a joke. So is the dictum 'Those who can, do; those who can't, teach; those who can't teach, go into administration,' though the third part may be just as true as the first two. In fact almost all education authorities regard successful teaching experience as an essential qualification for new entrants to administration.

Most of us quite like arranging and organizing things, and teaching itself is not always the unalloyed delight those outside it sometimes pretend. Still, there are plenty of opportunities today for administrative posts in the schools and colleges that can satisfy a taste for organization and ease the strain of actual teaching. Headships of large schools are nowadays just as rewarding financially as the senior posts in education offices and principalships of colleges often more so.

So it is hard to put a name to the elements in the make-up of a teacher, good at his job and likely to make progress in the profession, that make him turn instead to administration. Often curiosity is the nearest one can get: the wish to widen one's horizons and to take part in bigger events. Perhaps the desire may merely be one for greater variety of experience: perhaps it includes an element of wanting to do good on a bigger scale. There is plenty of room for cynicism about any of these, and plenty of scope for disillusionment, but taken together they seem to fit the facts.

Whatever the motives, the transition is likely to create suspicion in both worlds, the old and the new. For teachers may well feel towards a colleague who becomes an administrator the mingled envy and contempt of front-line troops for a comrade who successfully applies for a transfer to headquarters. Their concern thereafter is whether the neophyte has had enough battle experience to fit him for a career directed towards putting things right for those who are still at the front. On the other hand the new colleagues at base may not be too enthusiastic either. Within the education office the recruit is like a subaltern, knowing very little, and with ideas that may seem quite unrealistic to those he must, theoretically, lead. In other departments, particularly the treasurer's, his academic origins are a source of suspicion grounded in the extravagances associated with the impact of educational expenditure upon the rates.

Ambivalence

Perhaps it is fitting that entry to the world of educational administration should be so fraught with paradox. For the whole of the education officer's subsequent career will be marked by ambivalence; he will live in two worlds slipping uneasily from one to the other like an incompetent chameleon. It is not just that he has to deal with office matters on the one hand and the affairs of a separate profession on the other, though there is an inter-action between the two which gives educational administration a special flavour and special problems. He lives in the cross-fire of the demands of local government conditions and those of a costly and idealistic service. He is increasingly told that planning is the way to resolve this conflict, yet in neither of his two worlds has planning so far made any serious challenge to pragmatism as a way of life. His legitimate objectives are often obscured by tension between the decisions of the local council who employ him and the policy of the Government for the development of education nationally. Even his day-to-day decisions are complicated by the ambiguities of a service heavily endowed with legal and regulatory pronouncements yet demanding at every important point an approach that puts the needs of individuals first. Finally, both policy and practice demand expertise of the highest order yet the principle of lay control is firmly entrenched.

In a democracy, state education reflects rather than moulds public opinion. In emergent nations there may be earlier stages when standards of teaching and the production of constructive attitudes are the first consideration, but in a developed society freedom may count for more than efficient or highly skilled education. Of course we want both, but it does not need much imagination to see that democracy lags behind fascism so far as efficiency is concerned. We have chosen freedom first. A Royal Commission over a hundred years ago (The Taunton Report, 1868) said this: 'We are convinced that it is vain to expect thoroughly to educate the people of this country except by gradually inducing them to educate themselves.

3

Those who have studied the subject may supply the best guidance, and Parliament may be persuaded to make laws in accordance with their advice. But the real force, whereby the work is to be done, must come from the people. And every arrangement which fosters the interest of the people in the schools, which teaches the people to look on the school as their own, which encourages them to take a share in the management, will do at least as much service as the wisest advice and the most skilful administration.' And the White Paper on Educational Reconstruction, 1943, the forerunner of the 1944 Act, begins: 'The Government's purpose in putting forward the reforms described in this Paper is to secure for children a happier childhood and a better start in life.'

Neither document is concerned with developing an educational system as an aspect of national investment. In the Crowther Report of 1959 there is a significant change of tone: 'If we are to build a higher standard of living—and, what is more important, if we are to have higher standards in life—we shall need a firmer educational base than we have today. Materially and morally, we are compelled to go forward.' Since then the economic argument has been increasingly heard. The waste of talent is deplored not only on social but on material grounds and with greater expenditure on education the need for greater efficiency has grown.

The people's 'share in the management of the schools' has in practice been coupled with their responsibility for raising money from the rates. For thirty-two years from 1870 to 1902 this responsibility was entrusted to directly elected school boards, since then to the local authorities providing education as one of many services. In itself this is a practice entirely compatible with democratic government. The loss of efficiency through division of responsibility between central and local authority is far outweighed by the merits of local control.

But long before the state began to provide education the churches and other philanthropic bodies had done so. The dual system, adopted in 1870 and continued in modified form today, in which grants were given to voluntary schools and state schools were provided to fill the gaps, led to the continuation of existing boards of governors and the establishment of new ones, for state as well as voluntary schools. Again there can be no quarrel with the aim of securing support and encouragement for individual schools by interested local citizens. But an additional tier has been inserted into the governing structure and this can reduce efficiency still further. In county areas there is yet another tier, the divisional

4

executive, with delegated powers to manage particular areas. At what point does the balance between democracy and efficiency become tilted too far in one direction?

Quite apart from the structure of elected governing bodies the system poses another problem. Efficiency must to a great extent be connected with professional expertise whereas democratic control specifically and deliberately subordinates the professional to the elected layman. Perhaps bureaucracy is a greater evil but the education service has built-in democratic safeguards that, look at them how you will, tend towards inefficiency.

The administrator exists to make the system work, not to change it to suit his convenience. If his concern is that he is rendered less efficient by the system then he must try to see his own situation as a smaller-scale example of the total educational picture. It is undeniable that it would be more efficient to have standardized provision of all kinds of educational institution controlled by a central policy-making body. Yet each local education authority is free within broad limits to fix its own pattern. Democracy demands it.

This inter-play of local and national influence is another aspect of ambivalence for the education officer. National influence in education, relative to local power, has grown over the years. He who pays the piper calls the tune and the central government share of educational finance has steadily increased since the first grant of £20,000 in 1833. From the beginning of this century the state has generally found at least half of the total expenditure. By 1958 the share of local education costs had become about 60 per cent. In that year a general grant to local authorities for all services replaced the specific grant for education, but the removal of Ministry of Education control that was supposed to go with it was microscopic and specific financial dependence was replaced by the general dependence of local authorities on central government. Leaving out income from rents and trading services, local administrations in England and Wales between 1962 and 1967 got 52 per cent of their income from government grants. Although the change to the general grant system was supposed to make local authorities freer to spend their own money as they wished it made no real difference. And the rate support grant which replaced it in 1967 was designed to help the central government to control expenditure on all local services.

By far the costliest items in the local education budget are the salaries of teachers and the building of schools and colleges: both are controlled from Whitehall. The Burnham Committee which negotiates the salary scales was originally a joint negotiating committee of the local education authorities and the teachers' associations: the Secretary of State for Education and Science now has representatives on the committee and his view increasingly dominates the negotiations. The number of teachers each authority may employ is also controlled through a quota system operated by the Department. The number of new schools and colleges each authority may build is controlled by the Secretary of State and the standards to which they must be built are specified in great detail by his Department. The Government decides whether priority must be given to primary or secondary schools, to urban renewal or suburban overspill and it can direct other aspects of policy indirectly through the annual building programmes: for example, from 1966 only secondary schools fitting in with the national policy of comprehensive education could be built.

Thus no local education officer can help feeling very much involved in a national education movement. And yet the change from specific education grant to general grant in 1958, without affecting the degree of central control, increased the subordination of the education service to the local council. Naturally the fact that some 60 per cent of anything spent on education would be reimbursed had until then meant that the plans of education committees had rather more chance of success than those of less fortunate services. The freedom was like that of a wife with money of her own. When the specific grant went the situation changed, and education simply became the biggest and costliest amongst a number of services all of which had to be financed from the same pocket. Councils generally became less inclined to allow freedoms designed to take into account special factors appropriate to the education service. The powers of veto and revision exercised by finance committees and establishment committees have become particularly significant.

To talk of special factors may seem like merely special pleading yet there are reasons why education can legitimately demand special treatment. When this is not allowed, the education officer can find the gap betwen his two worlds hard to bridge. There are many examples. One may serve to illustrate how great the gulf can sometimes be. In the past schools were given money for books, stationery and materials after scrutiny by an official of their individual requests for specific items. Most education authorities later changed to a system in which so much per pupil was allowed to the school for each of these categories to be spent by the head at his discretion.

This seemingly modest change was in itself an important reform and one with implications for the work of the school, not just its accounts.

Now educational research and the views of good teachers have over the years demonstrated to even the most reactionary educationists that other media can be just as valuable as books in the educating process: for example, film strips, tapes, radio and television and records. Many heads have found that sometimes the amount allowed for books has been too much for a particular year but that they could have done with much more to spend on other materials and small equipment. Education officers have therefore suggested—and education committees have agreed—that the *per capita* allowances for books, stationery and materials should be amalgamated allowing the head to lay out his money to best advantage according to the particular needs of the moment.

Yet schemes like this have sometimes fallen foul of financial conventions. In the traditional pattern of budgeting expenditure is categorized according to types of resource—staff, buildings, equipment and so on—rather than the purpose they are supposed to serve. Current experiments with various forms of output budgeting which try to relate expenditure both to purpose and results may help to create a better climate for educational advance and incidentally give better value for money.

The example is a reminder that education committees and their officers have to justify policies, sometimes in detail, to those outside the service who control the purse-strings. The theory is admirable and it can often work well. Whether it does or not depends on the quality of the elected members and their officers.

One of the stock answers given to those who ask for more elbow-room to carry out the development of education that the nation needs is to say that with proper planning, with more intensive and more rational use of existing resources most of the problems could be solved. Treasurers are inclined to say it, although the conventions they sometimes support work against the notion. Economists call for long-term planning of education as a national investment. It looks easier from the outside than it really is.

The way the public education service has grown (with the central government always intent on saving money when projecting any reform and thus devising ingenious ways of thrusting responsibility upon local committees) is the classic way to ensure that what we get will cost more in the end. But democracy, as well as being less efficient and costing more in the end, is not easily reconcilable to long-term planning. As long as there are regular elections there can be no long-term plans for education in our kind of democracy.

What has to happen is something rather different. An agreed—or nearly agreed—objective has to emerge democratically before plans can be formulated. A typical pattern is something like this. An advisory committee is called together to report on a problem. The report is published. If it achieves a measure of support from educational opinion—including teachers' unions, local authorities, politicians and the general public—the Government tries to decide in the light of its current policies what it should do. Soundings are taken, kites are flown and a policy decision is made. Parliament, the Chancellor of the Exchequer and changing circumstances may all lead to modifications. With luck some part of the original plan may be put into practice, probably in differing ways to suit the circumstances of different local authorities. Then the process begins all over again with some other aspect.

In practice not every decision has even this amount of theory and planning in its ancestry. Comprehensive education, for instance, just emerged as a national policy. It is possible to regard this as a monstrous situation; a good example in fact of the need for long-term planning on sound theoretical grounds both educational and economic. Yet could such an issue be decided, in our country at any rate, in any other way? What kind of research could be undertaken to prove or disprove the validity of the comprehensive idea? What else than actual experience can show any valid results? What measure of agreement is there between the educators on the theoretical arguments? How can you separate the educational from the social aspects? How could the economist help to settle this one even if it were regarded as simply a question of getting the best return for national investment?

Even if we set aside the totalitarian implications of the notion of long-term planning we are left with a basic difficulty for the educational administrator. This centres upon the pragmatic nature of the British people. To some extent the conflict between the two worlds he must simultaneously inhabit, education and local government, can be seen as one between theory and practicalities. Yet this is an over-simplification for in truth both his worlds are essentially governed by pragmatism. The teacher in the classroom, who is and must remain at the centre of the educational stage, is certainly not one to be swept away by theory. In fact he is unlikely to be even influenced by theory unless he can be shown that it will work in practice. The same is true of local councillors.

The development of the education service depends on certain principles, too general to be called a plan, and too much concerned with social questions to be strictly educational. They are discussed and propounded by politicians, by teachers and by the electors. And they concern such things as the rights of human beings to have an education, and to be trained for a job, and the provision of equal opportunity for everyone. Every so often a measure of agreement emerges about the implications of these principles for a certain branch of education at a particular moment of time. When that moment comes the education officer has to seize the opportunity, first to clarify the issues and to make sure the implications are understood, then to suggest ways in which the principles can be put into practice.

Planning has to recognize these circumscribing factors, however depressing the thought may be to economists. Whether the basis of educational advance in a planned economy is social demand, man-power requirements or return for investment, it will always have to contend in a free society with the persistent amateurism and opportunism that regular, democratic elections foster. Embedded in the projects listed in the Inventory of Research Needs produced by UNESCO is the deceptively simple question 'How much should a nation spend on education?' Who, in this country, would be universally accepted as able to answer that question authoritatively? What principles would we use to determine the meaning of the word 'should'? What methods have we, or could we have, for finding an answer to the financial question even if the basis of approach were somehow agreed?

Better planning is needed, and there are ways in which advances can and should be made. They must however be compatible with the essential feature of educational administration: its account-ability to public opinion. The present system is the result of growth not planning, and the future is likely to be built through continued growth and adjustment. If an education service adequate to main-tain and strengthen the nation's economic position and bring a better life to its people is to be built, the factors the economists bring out must weigh heavily in the development. Yet if something even more precious is to be retained the essential principles on which the educa-tion service has rested must be unchanged.

Down to earth

It is time to come down from the clouds. Education is but one of many issues illustrating the dilemma of the conflicting needs of democracy and efficiency. Britain's search for a future role that is acceptable to the nation's conscience, appropriate to its resources yet in line with its past traditions, extends into every sphere of life. And though educationists believe that what they have to offer can play a leading part in shaping such a future they may perhaps be excused if they cannot themselves supply ready-made answers to such puzzling questions.

The education officer is for most of his working life concerned with what exists, the real world not the visionary products of wand-waving reformers. The teacher coming into administration is likely to find more mundane examples of the confusions inherent in the double life he has to lead. To what extent should he spend his time in the schools and colleges, to what extent in the office? What is the purpose of his school visits and what is his role when he gets there? Though these are down-to-earth questions they are by no means simple ones. The decision is not usually one for the young adminis-trator himself: the chief education officer will doubtless have a policy. Sometimes the policy will centre on keeping the beginner close to his desk, learning his new trade and performing the specific duties for which he has been appointed. Sometimes it will require the trainee (for that is what he is) to spend as much time as possible in the early days 'getting round the schools'.

There are some obvious advantages. Heads and administrators have to talk on the telephone and it is as well to know what is at the other end. It is courteous to present oneself to new colleagues. It is difficult if not impossible to make effective judgements or to give advice without forming a clear picture of the person and the environment with which you are dealing. It is necessary to get to know localities as well as just educational buildings, to get the feel of the cities and districts, to try to become part of them.

But there are also some less obvious but quite fundamental benefits. The relationship between schools and the office is a vital one, but as we shall see later, it is not a simple relationship. It changes over the years through individuals and institutions getting to know each other better and through changes in professional status, public esteem, and developing concepts of democratic government. Quite apart from this, at any given moment of time the education officer can stand in a different relationship to his colleagues in the schools depending on the circumstances that arise : a mistake in the office, trouble in the schools, a governors' meeting, consultation with teachers' unions, an application for a job—these are just a few of the situations in which teachers and administrators encounter each other every day, and there is a different relationship in each case.

If he is fortunate the new-comer will find that a programme of visits to schools has been arranged for him : experienced senior colleagues will know where the new man can best start and which visits should be deferred until later. Apart from the intrinsic interest of the visit and the valuable personal contact, other things will emerge. Without any doubt the head will wish to show his visitor round the school and to meet the staff. Developments and achievements will be pointed out. So will shortcomings. Indeed it is likely that the faulty roof in the science laboratory and the need for a new workshop will come up in the conversation early on. Opinions will be exchanged and requests will be made. The head may refer to a circular from the office and the administrator will see for himself any gap between writer's intention and reader's reception : or there may have been a letter sent in June and still unanswered in September. The administrator is launched, with a whole crop of things that seem important to his front-line colleague and some opportunities to be of service. When he returns to the office he will doubtless discover, in trying to remedy defects and to meet individual requests, some of the basic difficulties of administration— reconciling the individual with the general and the ideal with the attainable—and his task can begin. Next time he makes a visit he will know more about policies and possibilities and will be able to discuss problems, requests and complaints in that context.

As time goes on the visits may become, inevitably, less frequent; as he progresses in his career the requests, the complaints and the problems may come to him less directly and from many sources; but the basic process is the same, as intermediary between the requirements of the teaching process and the resources of the public purse. With growing confidence and experience he will add new, positive dimensions to the role—ideas, proposals for change, reorganization—but his two-eyed stance towards education and administration will still be necessary and, if he is successful, he must feel the pull from each of them equally all his working life.

It will be seen that there is a built-in opportunity in this situation for an adroit runner with the hare and hunter with the hounds. This is a question to some extent of conscience, to some extent of ordinary prudence. It is clearly not right, however tempting, to blame the committee and the system when with teachers, and to write down the teachers' attitude as irresponsible and extravagant

11

when with the committee : good administration will bring the committee and the teachers closer together not push them apart. At the merely prudential level hypocrisy and double-dealing once discovered will leave a credibility gap in every subsequent transaction.

Nor can the education officer choose to concentrate on either the educational or the administrative side of his job. He cannot take refuge in academic pursuits and leave the office to the junior staff. Still less can he bury himself in procedures, committee resolutions and the minutiae of the Department's building programme, and forget the existence of the schools and colleges it is his business to serve.

Some compromise has to be reached between what may be extreme and opposing points of view, and therein lies another danger. In seeking a middle way the education officer may appear to strike academic attitudes in the administrative world and on the other hand apply bureaucratic standards to educational issues. Then he is in a sorry state indeed.

The resolution of this kind of difficulty is not a matter which a few brisk rules can help. It is a question of judgement. Good judgement comes from intuition and experience. It can be helped by good training, and in the absence of any organized pre-entry training courses the responsibility falls on those who recruit young men and women fresh from teaching. They must give an opportunity to learn, to make mistakes and to profit from experience.

The inter-action of education and administration

What is the right relationship between the two elements? Clearly the two must be inter-related but not confused. To try to separate them is to forget the essential purpose of administration—to make good teaching possible. To confuse them is to do a service neither to the schools nor to the processes of government. Yet each must inter-act upon the other. If the administrator recognizes that clearly and tries to understand that it is a necessary and desirable process he will be half-way towards his goal. The important thing is first to distinguish the two elements and then to encourage their inter-action.

A simple and tangible example is the planning of new schools. In the past when discipline and formal instruction were the fundamental principles of education a central assembly hall surrounded by classrooms met the purpose, but the head of a modern primary school is likely to see the whole school as potential teaching space.

It may be capable of sub-division to allow working in groups; there may be messy areas, quiet corners and book nooks, but the aim will be flexibility. Primary schools have become places of enquiry, of excitement in learning, of individual endeavour, of change and enthusiasm. So the administrator must catch the spirit of the time, or even of coming time, and transmit it to the architect. New methods can be used in old buildings, but it is harder and the incentive is less. What matters in design is that educational needs come first. And the head and the education officer have a joint duty to try to ensure that any serious restrictions are overcome. Modification of the building, new equipment and ingenious methods of using what there is—all play their part in the struggle to see that the environment is not restrictive of the kind of education that is required.

The corollary is that very many administrative decisions have implications for education. These implications go beyond such straightforward matters as the number of staff allowed. They can affect the whole approach of a school to its educational work. We have referred earlier to capitation schemes which allow freedom to heads to lay out the available money to best advantage and have seen how the flexibility or otherwise of such a scheme can affect the kind of provision of books, equipment and materials, affecting in turn the kind of education it is possible to offer. If the sums of money set aside in the estimates are too tightly restricted in the range of items that can be bought this can have a deep and lasting impression on the school, perhaps confine it to traditional methods in spite of the convictions of the head and staff.

From this it will be clear that the education officer is concerned not merely with the smooth running of the machinery of government, nor with the provision and costs of education, but with its quality. His responsibility goes beyond the negative (though necessary) stage of purging his administrative habits of features likely to be harmful to the school: he must positively work to improve the quality of the school's work.

Now this responsibility is integral to his relationship with heads of schools and teachers generally. It is not the simple manager-employee relationship that it is sometimes thought to be. Neither, on the other hand, is it merely the administrator's function to supply the needs of the schools, or to act as a go-between from schools to education committee. He has a responsibility to the committee for securing education of the highest quality possible. He has to arrange in-service training for teachers; he has to see that the schools are given—and sometimes that they take—the best possible advice on educational matters; he has to give advice himself to heads and assistant teachers both in response to their queries and, sometimes, unasked; he is concerned with the appointment of teachers, particularly heads, and he is concerned with their performance. His ultimate responsibility is in fact to the children and their parents and it should be recorded that he will from time to time have to deal with complaints, not only about physical conditions, but about educational standards. Sometimes the answer is quantitative—a teacher short perhaps—and his problem is straightforward, though not easy. Sometimes, however, it is to do with quality and then he will require not merely patience and understanding or the skills and attributes of a good administrator, but sufficient knowledge of and concern for education itself to form a judgement about the causes of any deficiency and about how to start putting it right.

If there ever was a service, then, whose administration required something more than management skills, it is education. Although, as we shall see later, there might well be scope, particularly in large offices, for men with other professional skills, such as accountancy or even architecture, and although valuable and devoted service is often given by lay officers, nevertheless the direction, control and leadership of educational administration must come from professional educationists. Direct experience as a teacher or a lecturer is without doubt the most valuable background for an education officer. It is not only knowledge of education and its problems that he will gain that way (though this may be considerable) but knowledge and understanding of the problems and satisfactions of the teaching profession with whom he will afterwards have to work. And perhaps even more valuable than that will be the simple fact that he cared enough about education to make it his career from the very outset. This understanding and concern are the two qualities he must bring with him if he is ever to get the special feel of educational administration.

2

The context

To understand what education officers do and why they do it we have to consider the context in which they operate. This chapter does not set out to give a detailed account of the education system of Britain, but an indication of the legal and formal background of its administration. It will be selective, for too much detail would obscure the issue.

The education system

However brief, this must be a motion picture. The government of education is constantly evolving along with society itself so that any suggestion of the permanent and immutable would be misleading. Perhaps the first thing for any existing or potential administrator to remember is that he must be adaptable. The 1944 Education Act has to be seen not as a definitive document but as one stage in a developing system. Then again local government generally is in the process of change, both in boundaries and in methods of working. New relationships between central and local government are being evolved, and regional influences are growing.

In other ways, too, simple description of 'a system' would be misleading. Our traditions are those of variety and freedom, decentralization of administration, strong involvement of voluntary agencies and grass-roots freedom for teachers to develop their own curricula and teaching methods. And although the same general policy is being followed everywhere in the United Kingdom, there are variations in Scotland, Northern Ireland and to a lesser extent

Wales. Concentration here on England and Wales is not intended to minimize the importance of Scottish educational traditions, in many ways in advance of those south of the Border, or those of Northern Ireland. It is a question of simplification, bearing in mind first that the bulk of the population is in England and Wales, and second that the aim is to get beyond the structure to examine what goes on inside it.

Even if we wished we could hardly regard the 1944 Act as definitive: it is essentially a triumph of British compromise. It has the gift of appearing to look different according to the angle from which it is approached. Thus it can fairly be stated that the most important clause is Section 1 which provides for the Secretary of State 'to promote the education of the people of England and Wales and the progressive development of institutions devoted to that purpose', but on the other hand the Department of Education and Science does not provide and control educational establishments directly. The local education authorities can point out that whatever the Secretary of State's powers and duties these stem like their own from an Act of Parliament: the local education authorities are not mere outposts of a centrally directed empire.

The very same Section 1 gives the Secretary of State the duty 'to secure the effective execution by local authorities, under his control and direction, of the national policy', but then goes on to qualify 'national policy' as one 'for providing a varied and comprehensive educational service in every area'.

Then again the religious question, which had bedevilled English education since the time of the Civil War and had been partially resolved by the establishment under the 1870 Act of the dual system was modified by skilful compromise to meet the modern situation. The White Paper on Educational Reconstruction in 1943 put it nicely: 'Discussions carried on in recent months with the many interests concerned have satisfied the Government that there is a wide increase of agreement that voluntary schools should not be abolished but rather that they should be offered further financial assistance, accompanied by a corresponding extension of public control. . . .' Thus the churches had a choice between 'aided' status (which allowed them to continue with much the same rights as in the past but paying a proportion of the costs of new buildings, improvements and repairs) and 'controlled' status (which cost them nothing but required them to give up certain rights).

Section 76 of the Act deserves special mention as an illustration of the principle of compromise. It has been widely quoted by parents, particularly in relation to comprehensive reorganization : 'Pupils are to be educated in accordance with the wishes of their parents.' But the full text says : 'In the exercise and performance of all powers and duties conferred and imposed upon them by this Act the Secretary of State and local authorities shall have regard to the general principle that, so far as is compatible with the provision of efficient instruction and training and the avoidance of unreasonable public expenditure, pupils are to be educated in accordance with the wishes of their parents.' The reservations make a difference.

In truth the Act is so hedged about with ambiguities and so modified in practice by financial and other external controls that on matters of government it is unwise to take it literally. Section 68 is an example. It confers powers on the Secretary of State to over-rule any local education authority whether they have delegated powers under the Act or not if they 'have acted or are proposing to act unreasonably'. If this power were used freely—and nothing in the section recommends limitations on its use—the relations between central and local government would be very different from what they are. In fact even threats to use it have been extremely rare, and only unimaginable conduct by an authority would allow a Secretary of State who invoked it to escape charges of dictatorship. On the other hand it may well be that this reserve power has sometimes prevented what might have amounted to unreasonable conduct by local authorities.

People are sometimes cynical about the conventional description of the way the system works as a partnership, but there is no better metaphor; and if all the partners are not equal then it is difficult to see how they could be. The partners are many, as we shall notice, and their theoretical powers may not be the same as their influence, which in our system is just as important and occasionally more so. Since our whole constitution is proudly hailed as unwritten, and its application is based largely on case law, it would be surprising if the same did not apply to the education service.

The Act established a Minister and Ministry of Education, later to become the Secretary of State and the Department of Education and Science. It prescribed a three-stage system, primary, secondary and further education, the first two to be provided free. Nursery education was to be available for children from the age of two, with compulsory primary schooling from five to between ten-and-a-half and twelve years, and compulsory secondary education thereafter to fifteen and eventually sixteen years of age.

Primary and secondary schools established and maintained by

local education authorities were called county schools; those maintained but not established by LEAs were called voluntary schools,
with either aided or controlled status. Independent schools were
to be registered and open to inspection. The LEAs were to provide
special education for the handicapped, ancillary services such as
school meals, milk, clothing in needy cases, transport and board
and lodging, medical and dental inspection and some treatment.

Further education was to include full-time and part-time education for people over compulsory school age, including cultural and
recreational provision. There was to be a national system for training
teachers in colleges maintained by local education authorities and
voluntary bodies. The LEAs were given power to make grants to
individuals for schooling, further education, teacher training and
university education, and to universities and certain other educational bodies. The universities remained outside this system, though
their Education Departments trained teachers and they were the
base for Institutes of Education controlling the content of all teacher
training. Certain other powers were given to the LEAs by other
legislation such as the Employment and Training Act 1948 which
created the Youth Employment Service.

Local education authorities

Local education authorities are strictly the local councils not their
education committees, though they are required to appoint such
committees, and to consider reports from them before making
decisions about education, and to appoint chief education officers.
At first there were specific grants for education from the central
government but from 1958 this financial contribution was in the
form of a general grant, later called the Rate Support Grant, to
the local council to be used at its discretion for all its services.

Since 1902 education has been amongst the services administered
by local authorities. Until the second world war there were only
minor reforms in local government but since 1945 many attempts
have been made at full-scale reorganization. The London Government Act 1963 replaced over 100 local authorities by the Greater
London Council and 32 London Boroughs (plus the City). Twenty
of these became responsible for their own education, with populations around a quarter of a million. Education in the remainder
became the responsibility of the Inner London education authority
with a population of over 3 million: this is a committee of the
GLC with extensive delegated powers.

Elsewhere everyone, except the authorities themselves, has tended to agree that some are too small to provide the necessary resources for local government. By 1969 there were 60 county and 82 county borough councils with populations ranging from about 18,000 to over 2 million in England and Wales which made it difficult to conceive of any general principles of partnership between central and local government. The county borough—county division by then bore no relation to either people's living and working habits or administrative convenience.

Successive local government commissions found their terms of reference too narrow to cope with the problem of producing authorities that were of appropriate size for a wide range of functions and that had social and administrative coherence. In Wales the Government had decided by 1969 to replace thirteen counties and four county boroughs by five counties, all but one over 300,000 population, and three county boroughs, with populations from 113,000 to 289,000, but then decided that further exploration was needed. In this they were influenced by the more radical solutions felt to be needed in England, where a Royal Commission in 1969 recommended 58 unitary (all-purpose, town-and-country) authorities averaging 500,000 population, and 3 metropolitan areas for the Birmingham, Liverpool and Manchester conurbations with education the responsibility of metropolitan districts averaging 400,000 population. (Characteristically a Royal Commission for Scotland set up at the same time and with similar terms of reference recommended a different pattern based on seven regions. In Northern Ireland still different solutions have emerged through consultation with existing local authorities.) The only certain thing about the outcome of these attempts at reform is that education authorities will in future tend to be bigger and fewer in number.

Their main duties are to:

1 provide full-time primary and secondary education in schools sufficient in number, character and equipment to give to all pupils instruction and training appropriate to their ages, abilities and aptitudes. This includes nursery schools, special schools and boarding education as appropriate;
2 maintain approved voluntary schools;
3 maintain all schools according to standards specified by the Secretary of State;
4 make instruments and articles of management or government for county primary and secondary schools;

19

5   produce development plans for their areas;
6   make arrangements for religious instruction according to the Act;
7   ascertain what special education treatment is needed;
8   ensure that all parents cause their children to be suitably educated;
9   provide medical inspection and treatment;
10 provide milk and meals according to regulations;
11 secure adequate facilities for further education, full-time and part-time, including leisure-time activities;
12 set up county colleges if ever they are authorized by the Secretary of State;
13 carry out directions of the Secretary of State requiring them to provide or help to maintain institutions for training of teachers.

Their powers include :

1   establishing new schools, maintaining as county schools schools formerly independent or voluntary, and ceasing to maintain schools;
2   grouping schools under one management;
3   controlling secular instruction in county schools, and voluntary schools (except aided secondary schools);
4   controlling the appointment of teachers (except for special arrangements, notably those for religious education in voluntary schools);
5   controlling, within limits, the use of voluntary school premises;
6   providing board and lodging, clothing and making other special arrangements for educating children with special needs;
7   regulating the part-time employment of school-children;
8   inspecting, through their officers, educational establishments maintained by them;
9   making grants and meeting expenses of pupils and students for whose education they are responsible;
10 conducting or assisting research;
11 assisting universities and certain other educational bodies;
12 accepting gifts for educational purposes;
13 compulsorily purchasing land required for approved educational purposes;
14 providing a Youth Employment Service.

There is no doubt, then, about the very broad powers and duties of the local education authorities. The 1944 Act requires them 'so far as their powers extend, to contribute towards the spiritual, moral, mental and physical development of the community by securing that efficient education shall be available to meet the needs of the population of their area'.

It is significant, too, that the Department of Education and Science does not maintain and operate educational establishments. That is in the main the duty of the local education authorities though there are exceptions.

The qualification is necessary. For some aspects of education the LEAs have no responsibilities, notably the universities and the independent schools. Even within their sphere of influence they share responsibilities with certain other statutory and very many non-statutory agencies. For example, by 1967, of the 22,831 primary schools maintained by LEAs over a third were provided by voluntary bodies, including 6,644 by the Church of England and 1,873 by the Roman Catholic Church; and of the 5,729 secondary schools, 526 were Roman Catholic and 217 Church of England, with 247 others. This is quite apart from the 179 grammar schools receiving direct grant from the Department of Education and Science.

Of some 800 maintained special schools about one in seven is voluntary, and of course the voluntary origins of social work, like education, are shown in the continuation of voluntary child guidance clinics and similar child services. Voluntary influence is strong in youth and community work where LEAs have provided a local framework rather than a fully-fledged service.

Since 1889 the local authorities have been prominent in providing vocational further education, and the bulk of present provision is theirs; all but a handful of over 700 major establishments. Over 7,500 evening institutes cater for nearly a million and a half adult education students, though almost a quarter of a million others attend classes organized by the WEA and the universities, quaintly known as Responsible Bodies.

Relationships with the various partners are complex, and teacher training provides a formidable example. More than 200 institutions are concerned, about three-fifths being maintained by LEAs, including as well as colleges of education Art Training Centres in certain colleges of art and training departments in technical colleges. Over fifty are voluntary, sponsored by the churches but receiving grants from the DES covering approved running costs and similar capital grants to those for voluntary schools. Some 30 are university departments of education. Though the responsibility for ensuring the supply of teachers, balanced to meet the requirements of the various sectors, is that of the Secretary of State, responsibility as to standards is effectively that of the universities. Area Training Organizations representing universities, LEAs and the training institutions, serviced (except in Cambridge) by university-based Institutes or Schools of Education, are responsible for schemes of training. There can be fewer better examples of the checks and balances in our system.

Control by the Department of Education and Science

Yet the two main influences on the education officer's work are the local council and the Department of Education and Science. The Local Government Manpower Committee in 1951 set out six key points on which the Secretary of State must be satisfied in relation to local education authorities:

1 that educational facilities and ancillary services are provided in sufficient quantity and variety;
2 that educational establishments and ancillary services are well managed, equipped, staffed and maintained;
3 that the proper freedom of parents, teachers and other third parties is secured;
4 that the qualifications of teachers and medical officers are such as to satisfy proper requirements to safeguard their and the children's interests;
5 that the fees charged and awards and allowances made are such as are necessary and appropriate;
6 that the provision of education premises satisfies essential standards.

Educational legislation comes from Parliament: not only the main Bills but subsequent regulations are laid before Parliament. The function of the DES is to see that this legislation is carried out. The Department does this through Statutory Instruments, through day-to-day contact with local education officers, through Her Majesty's Inspectors, through building programmes and through financial control.

The shelves of every education office bend gently under the weight of Statutory Instruments (Rules and Regulations on major matters), Administrative Memoranda (on questions of detail) and Circulars (interpreting policy). That they are not discussed here is not a mark of their lack of importance, but a question of space. They exist and they can be consulted.

Regulations enter into the daily life of the education officer rather less than might be supposed. To some extent this reflects the degree of local freedom in the system. To a large extent it is because often they appear to spell out what would have happened whether they existed or not.

Sometimes they seem not to add much to the sum of human knowledge : for example, the Further Education Regulations 1959 state happily, 'A person shall not be refused admission to or excluded from any establishment or from any course of instruction . . . on other than reasonable grounds.' It is difficult to know what sort of person would be influenced by that one.

The word 'reasonable' crops up quite a lot in the regulations, so it is not surprising to find that much discussion, consultation and even argument goes on between officers of the Department and of the local education authority. At the local end the officers concerned will be the chief education officer and his senior colleagues (although others may be involved at a lower level on specific points of detail) as well as architects, medical officers and other experts. At the Department the officer concerned may be a specialist in one of the branches, or an executive or even a clerical officer on some specific issue, but on important issues he will be a member of the administrative Civil Service. Each branch of the Department is headed by an Under-Secretary, but the normal routine contact with an LEA will be through a Territorial Officer, traditionally graded as a Principal but recently tending to be of the executive grade. He will deal himself with what he can and refer matters beyond his scope to the Assistant Secretary in charge of the branch concerned. The Territorial Officer system means that a regular and humanizing contact is possible with someone familiar with the circumstances of the region.

The familiarity is unlikely to come entirely or even largely from direct contact with the area. The administrative officers and executive officers are neither expert in education nor able to travel about the country very much. Their information tends to come from Her Majesty's Inspectors who cover the area and in fact live in it. Historically these men and women are best known for their role in carrying out formal inspections at the request of the Department (or the local authority) but it was never the whole of their work and this function has now ended. Increasingly they are concerned with advising the Department on a whole range of things concerning their area.

It is possible to take different views of their value. They perform very good service in organizing short courses for teachers in their own specialist subjects and in advising schools (particularly in smaller authorities who have no specialist advisers of their own). As local advisers to the Department they are of course very valuable. Though their information may not be quite as good as that which could be supplied by the Authority it is obviously likely to be more objective. In further education their specialization in a wide range of technical subjects is undoubtedly useful even to the biggest authorities and the Regional Staff Inspector for Technical Education performs the specific and not very popular function of approving or disallowing applications to put on new advanced courses. It is worth bearing in mind that the Inspectorate are the only people in the Department's service who have had professional experience in education, so there can be no doubt of the influence they have.

The Department exercises specific control, detailed and by now irksome, over local expenditure on new educational buildings and on improvements to existing ones. The Building Code describing all the procedures, regulations and cost limits occupies some 200 pages of small print and is subject to regular amendment. This is a very brief summary.

First, standards have been set to which new schools and colleges must be built throughout the country: they cover such things as sites, minimum areas for buildings and playing fields, minimum teaching areas and dining accommodation. For schools these are based on formulae according to the numbers and ages of pupils; for colleges of education, colleges of further education and youth clubs, standards are approved individually for each project. Then a cost limit is set which must not be exceeded: for schools this is again according to a formula based on the number and age of pupils; for other projects, which have to be designed for a wide range of local and specialist requirements, a different approach is needed. A standard cost per square foot of accommodation is fixed, varying according to the type of construction required, and applied to an agreed schedule of accommodation derived from the authorized standards. The Department produce *Building Bulletins* giving guidance on making the best use of available resources and suggesting ideas. They also offer information and advice from architects and HMI who have specialized in planning educational buildings. The code lays great stress on the value of informal consultation at every stage.

But before a new building can be planned it has to find a place in a *building programme*. Each year the Secretary of State announces how much money can be spent nationally on schools, further education, teacher training and youth service projects, and invites local education authorities to make proposals for inclusion in them. These are the *major building programmes* for projects normally costing over £20,000 each. The Secretary of State indicates what kind of projects are to be given priority—whether secondary or primary, for instance, urban or rural—and he may divide the amount up between a *main building programme* (designed to meet basic needs, such as new schools where there is increased population, or replacement of bad, old buildings) and *special programmes* such as that announced, later withdrawn and then reinstated, for raising the school leaving age. There are entirely separate major programmes for schools, further education, teacher training and on a much smaller scale the youth service. The Department decide, building by building, what can be included in each programme.

Apart from these major projects an annual sum is set aside nationally for minor capital works which may be built at the authority's discretion within a sum fixed each year according to the Department's estimate of local needs. There is a combined allocation for schools, further education and colleges of education.

The first thing to be noticed is that these building programmes are not allocations of money from central to local funds. Contrary to popular belief no money changes hands. The Secretary of State states how much the local authorities may spend of their own money. In effect it is the Government's method of controlling the total capital investment which it will allow on educational building.

No doubt this annual sum is intended to bear some relation to the physical needs of the education service, but it is much more readily understood if it is regarded as a measure of what the country's economic circumstances seem to require. Those who advocate long-term planning need look no further than the building programme arrangements to see how far we are from anything resembling even middle-distance planning. It is an annual lottery, fluctuating according to immediate pressures. The gamble is not merely in the unpredictable allocations that are made; an even worse feature is the 'stop-go' pattern. If times are hard then an announcement will be made that all work not actually started by a certain date must be re-submitted for further consideration according to new criteria. At other times—for instance if there is a threat of unemployment—telephone messages from the Department will tell certain authorities that if they can start projects before a given date authority will be given outside the normal programmes.

Perhaps the recurrent but eccentric cycle of glut and famine explains why after a quarter of a century's experience local education authorities are still subject to such detailed control of their building work. With set standards for premises, set cost limits and every kind of advice available to them it is hard to think why else authorities (who have after all highly qualified architects, advisers and administrators of their own) should not now be given much more discretion to determine local priorities. Many people think we have now reached the stage when more coherent planning and thus better value for money could be achieved if the reins were loosened.

The local government background

Control of education takes places locally as well as centrally. Rates are levied by councils on occupiers of premises and land to meet the cost of all local government services: the rate is based on the value of property not the prosperity of its owners. Consequently if the council wants more income it must put up the rate, unlike say an income tax in which the more you earn the more you pay. The last thing any council wants to do is increase the rates, but to avoid this it must either trim its services or get more money from the central government. More money from the government, even if granted, inevitably lessens local independence. Education is in the awkward position of being far the costliest local service: over half of local expenditure is needed nowadays. It is not hard to see, therefore, where councils look first when economies have to be made. The rate support grant, the government's contribution to local funds, is for all services with no amount specifically set aside for education. The council, not the education committee, decide how much of it should be given to education and how much to other services.

The local councillors are the proper people to entrust with decisions of this kind, and, in theory at any rate, it frees local services from central government control on specific issues. Yet to be the biggest brother in a family undergoing hard times is an unenviable role. Apart from the sheer size of the service, there are other factors. First, national pressures for the expansion of education are considerable: from the many reports describing deficiencies and outlining reforms; from the public more than ever conscious of its vital importance to their children; from the teachers claiming an increasing share in the national prosperity; from the Government itself. The present financial system makes it difficult to maintain standards, let alone improve them. Second, educational provision is different in kind from that of roads or houses. Beyond the physical provision of schools or teachers there are intangibles and the financial requirements of an education committee must take them into account. Considered in themselves they may well seem like luxuries, though the purposes they serve are essential. A child's attendance at a field study course might well be thought less important than a water-tight roof over a council house. Yet unless education has quality it is valueless. Comparison of specific issues can distort the picture.

The key figures in this situation are the finance committee and the treasurer. County councils are required by law to have a finance committee and in practice every education authority has one. The chief financial officer (usually the same person as the treasurer) is the authority's adviser on everything with financial implications, so that, depending on the degree of delegation to the education committee, he may be involved in the most detailed matters within the education service. Some authorities delegate fully to the education committee; that is, they approve an agreed sum to be spent each year and then allow the committee to administer it as they wish. At the other extreme some authorities delegate nothing so that every resolution of the committee becomes merely a recommendation requiring approval by the council: in these authorities the finance committee usually have to approve every recommendation involving expenditure or a large proportion of them.

Education cannot claim special privileges: like other social services its share of the total resources must depend on the consensus of public opinion which local finance committees are intended to reflect. Freedom for educationists to allocate those resources is vitally necessary if education is not to stagnate: on the other hand local councils need some yard-stick to measure the value for money education services provide and to help them determine how much to allocate.

Perhaps the gap can be bridged in future through output or programme-planning-budgeting. PPB as it is called has been used in the USA on defence and in Canada on a wider scale, and is beginning to be considered here both nationally and locally. In this system money is allocated to programmes with carefully defined objectives and with built-in methods of evaluating performance and impact-measures. The distance between this kind of thinking and what goes on in a primary school classroom is fairly considerable but unless these broad principles, or something like them, can be applied to the education service the financial future is bleak indeed.

Most councils have an establishment committee, a body whose function it is to approve any additions to staff, other than teachers, to negotiate through national bodies or locally, salaries, wages and conditions of service, to deal with leave of absence, motor car allowances and similar things, and latterly, to undertake organization and methods surveys. There is no need to emphasize how important such a committee can be in the life of an education officer, not merely because of its impact on the headquarters staff itself, but also because it is likely to take into its province all the clerks, welfare assistants, school nurses, laboratory and workshop technicians in schools and colleges, groundsmen, doctors, psychologists, school welfare officers, careers officers, cooks, caretakers, porters, drivers and so on that an education authority must have. Again it is hard to find fault with the theory that all departments should be treated alike and that the ratepayers should have the benefit of a standardized, well-regulated system. Yet in education the provision of ancillary staff is not simply a matter of finding bodies to do the jobs that otherwise would not get done: it is inextricably bound up with the quality of education.

The education committee is a great provider, a great employer, a great controller of institutions. To have detailed scrutiny of financial and establishment decisions by external forces is in effect to do many jobs twice or three times over, to deny the managers the resources they need and to deny them the freedom to allocate these resources in the way most suited to their service. It also breeds an attitude of leaving it to someone else that is fatal to any enterprise. Thus an education committee that knows its decisions on finance or other matters are subject to fierce control by others is inclined to sit back and approve proposals on the nod, secure in the knowledge that others will take the unpleasant decisions. The previous chapter emphasized the close inter-relationship of the academic and the administrative in the education service and pointed out the educational implications of even the simplest administrative decision. To encourage the neglect of this fact by reducing the influence of the education officer and his committee on these key sectors of finance and staff is unfortunate and potentially dangerous.

Discretion

What is the total effect of all these factors on the discretion exercised by education committees? The control of the Department of Education and Science through finance is not as effective as it might be. The rate support grant system robs it of much of the sensitivity it might have since it can only encourage or inhibit in a limited way by financial means. For most of the education service there is no way the DES can give a direct incentive to spend money on what are considered desirable national objectives. The building programmes act as an incentive only in so far as authorities are willing to spend their own money, so that in a sense the system can succeed only as long as the total amount of building allowed is less than authorities want to provide.

There are certain exceptions to this negative and generalized approach and they operate in an interesting way. Not all local education authorities maintain colleges of education for the training of teachers. Yet they all benefit from the training and the Department are of course anxious to maintain and regulate the supply. So the total cost of running these colleges is pooled: it is added together and the costs are then shared out amongst all authorities according to their school population. The authorities running the colleges are paid back their actual running costs, and simply pay their share on the same basis as everyone else. So there is an incentive to maintain colleges of education and to spend money on them: if an authority has its own college it can expect to recruit many of its products and in running the college it knows that all the other LEAs will have to help out with the costs.

Similarly not all authorities maintain colleges of further education that offer advanced level courses. Advanced further education is another matter of great national concern. So the Department control the provision of these courses and operate a pooling system to finance them. Again the running costs are reimbursed, the national bill is totalled and shared out (on a slightly different but similar formula) amongst all authorities. It does not take much imagination to see the inflationary tendency of this method: there is a general impression that nobody pays.

The only direct and positive financial incentive in the education service comes from outside sources—notably the 75 per cent of approved expenditure of the Youth Employment Service which is met by the Department of Employment and Productivity.

Some impression of the limits of financial freedom for an educa-

tion committee comes from analysis of the annual revenue estimates
to see how the expenditure is built up.

Item	Expenditure	Comments
Teachers' salaries including superannuation and national insurance	45·0%	The Burnham Committee determines salary levels (with some local discretion over above-scale allowances). The number of teachers employed (in schools) is largely determined by a quota fixed by the DES
Other salaries and wages	15·0%	Most scales are fixed by national bodies. Numbers are controlled by Establishment Committee
Premises and grounds : repair and maintenance	02·5%	To some extent discretionary but a certain minimum is of course essential
Fuel, Light, Water, Cleaning Materials	03·5%	To some extent discretionary but a certain minimum is of course essential
Rent and rates	03·5%	Inevitable
Debt charges	10·5%	Inevitable
Food, milk etc.	04·0%	Inevitable
Adjustments with other authorities	01·0%	Inevitable
Aid to pupils and students	07·5%	Mostly paid according to national scales : in large part according to national regulation
Equipment; books, stationery and materials	04·5%	
Furniture, repair and replacement	00·3%	
Improvements to buildings and furniture	00·7%	
Other expenses	02·0%	
	100·0%	

These figures are approximate and incomplete (they exclude the
Youth Employment Service and omit contributions to the services
financed by nationally pooled expenditure) but they show that a

great deal of expenditure has to be laid out according to conditions made by others than the education committee itself. Some sixty per cent goes on salaries and the next biggest element is debt charges on the new buildings that have been put up, which is quite inevitable and cumulative expenditure. Apart from this and grants and awards to students no individual item amounts to 5 per cent of the whole.

The heads of revenue expenditure under which there is much real discretion are few. Within the capital estimates the controlling factor for almost all of the expenditure is what is allowed by national building programmes. Of course there is still scope for careful budgeting and costing : the discretionary elements may be a small percentage but may still cover large sums of money; there is flexibility even with the terms of Burnham Reports and the teachers' quota system; finance and establishment committees are not always intransigent. Furthermore, local education authorities play a leading part in formulating the national schemes (such as the quota) which limit their individual discretion. And so long as there is reasonable financial support by central government for local councils the controls are not crippling. Understanding clerks, treasurers and establishment officers can make burdens that are theoretically intolerable quite light in practice. The special needs of education are better understood and tolerated by local finance committees than the strict logic of the situation might suggest.

Yet the over-riding impression is of a precarious, indirect, insensitive and cumbersome method of financing education. In any severe cutback of grants to local authorities education must perforce suffer most, whatever the plans the Secretary of State has in mind for the service. A specific percentage grant for education seems to many educationists a more effective and realistic way of provid-ing the developments the people expect. There are strong counter-arguments, but whatever system is used the issue is not simply one of how much money is allocated to education : the service must have more freedom within the limitations of broadly based assess-ments of financial need if it is to do the job the country expects.

Co-operation with other local government services

If these issues of freedom and finance can be settled there are clear advantages in including education within the local government framework. Public accountability is especially important in such a personal service and we have not yet discovered any better way of achieving it than by locally elected bodies. The pooling of resources for architectural, financial and legal services also makes good sense: including education often means that services which otherwise would not be an economic proposition become available to other branches. And, of course, many of the other services are closely related to education.

Perhaps the most influential partners are the Planning committees. The Town & Country Planning Acts give them wide powers over the use made of land and buildings which in turn gives them great influence in shaping the future development of society. Apart from controlling changes in the existing use of land they must decide the kind of development most suited to particular districts—residential, industrial, commercial, agricultural. Their development plans set out the programme for shaping the area in the future. Education committees must therefore find sites acceptable to planning committees for any new projects. The complexities of land acquisition are a sufficient reason in themselves for close co-operation with the education service as a large provider of buildings and playing fields. But beyond the purely physical questions education must play a large part in local plans for community development. In a democracy this must involve active participation of local residents in decisions affecting their future, so that the best planning committees will be much concerned to foster local community associations and similar organizations. Here is an obvious point of contact with education authorities whose youth and community committees are also concerned to work with and through this kind of district organization.

Housing is a major factor in the redevelopment of the decaying centres of towns and of overspill into suburban and rural areas. The education and housing committees must co-operate if there are to be schools, youth clubs, colleges for new housing developments. The timing of building operations by housing and education departments is crucial, and so, before that, is the calculation of the number of children likely to be in the new houses. A change of policy by the housing committee about the size of family it admits to its properties can result in serious overcrowding—or under-use—in the schools. In any event schools may be put to varied use in new housing estates. Families with young children are usually the first to be rehoused, and infant and junior school places are required. By the time they have grown older there may well be much smaller numbers of younger children—families don't go on growing—and there may be a surplus of accommodation. It is not unknown for an education authority to provide somewhat fewer secondary school places than are needed and to use former infants' schools as annexes to the secondary schools. This is a difficult exercise which may at the best of times tend to over- or under-provision for an area's long-term needs, so close collaboration between housing and education is essential. The collaboration often extends to joint planning of, for example, play centres for young children and community centres which may be built by housing committees as part of the amenities of a new estate and then staffed by the education authority.

Local education authorities are also concerned with libraries, the arts, sports and recreation, for which there may be separate local committees. The public library service is one of the least appreciated but most indispensable sides of local government. In some authorities the libraries are the responsibility of the education committee, but in any event co-operation is likely to extend from boxes of books delivered and changed regularly in schools or provided for teachers' courses to joint operation of technical information services with colleges of further education. Art galleries and museums, particularly in large urban authorities where there are large collections, play a similar part, and they may employ schools officers to arrange special programmes of visits and instruction and operate art or museum loan schemes.

Parks and Baths committees, too, have functions in common with education. As with housing, in county boroughs co-operation is easier (because in counties these functions are the responsibility of the minor authorities not the county council) and may even extend to the Parks Department actually maintaining school playing fields. Whatever the administrative arrangements there is clearly a need to make full use of all the facilities, public parks by schools and school fields by the public. Swimming baths, schools and public, also need to be used in co-operation, and the expertise of baths managers and their staffs can be a valuable asset to the education committee in planning swimming coaching programmes.

It is, of course, the social element in education that links it with the work of other local committees. This appears at its strongest in relation to the Health and Children's services: each has, like education, a concern for the well-being of the community and particularly the under-privileged part of it. In this part of local councils' work, because it is intensely personal and the problems often intangible or intractable, progress often appears slower than elsewhere. It is not made easier by the multiplicity of agencies, voluntary and statutory, local and national, each with a finger in the pie. The responsibility of the state for social welfare has only recently been accepted and the full extent of the responsibility is only gradually being determined and there is as yet no clear national policy. Yet social, psychological and physical factors are inextricably mixed with educational progress. Co-operation is essential, especially when the governmental processes are so tangled.

3

The committee structure

Ambrose Bierce has this entry in his *Devil's Dictionary*: 'PUBLIC, n. The negligible factor in problems of legislation.' If you equate 'the public' with 'elected representatives of the people' there is no neglect of the public in the education service. Elaborate safeguards are built in to the system to ensure the democratic control and direction of education. Yet, perhaps because of the very profusion of these safeguards, members of the public may well feel excluded from contact with the real sources of authority. To trace these sources is a difficult operation, for in one sense there are none. Even in theory the inter-play of roles of the many partners in education is complex: in practice it is more so, for the unwritten, the implicit and the understood are all-important.

Sir Edward Playfair has put forward (in *The Listener*, 8th February, 1968) an interesting theory about why the reform of the public services everyone talks about never seems to happen. 'Can it be,' he says, 'that we already have roughly the kind of government which we want, and that efficiency is not very popular? . . . The contemporary taste, a generation after the war, is for rather a lot of rather weak government.' If this is so the public's needs are well supplied in education. The partnership between central government, education authorities and the teaching profession is valuable, but of course a partnership weakens the authority of each of the partners. The existence of so many education authorities helps to provide varied services to meet different local circumstances, but it also means weaker individual authorities than if there were only a few. Consequently the authorities must join together, both nationally and regionally, in all kinds of formations to co-ordinate policy. This again diffuses the sources of authority. The legal requirement that there shall be education committees, divisional executives and governors and managers introduces democratic control at every level, but quite apart from its effect on efficient administration it sets up a chain of government that is leisurely in its approach and painstaking but unselective in operation.

The education committee

One can claim no more for the education committee as a starting point in an analysis of democratic control of education than this: it is the body through which a local council exercises, within its own limited sphere, its policy for education. We have seen something of the limitations imposed on councils and by them on education committees. To this we must add that governors, managers and divisional executives also have powers, and that in practice most education committee decisions are formal confirmations of sub-committee recommendations.

The 1944 Act requires each local education authority to appoint an education committee. LEAs may combine, if the Secretary of State agrees, to form joint education committees for some of their functions; for example running a large technical college. These are rare, though an important exception is the Joint Education Committee for Wales and Monmouthshire which deals with a number of matters requiring a co-ordinated policy.

The composition of the committee is subject to Ministerial approval: it must have a majority of elected members but must also have as co-opted members persons experienced in education. Many committees also co-opt representatives of the teaching profession, the churches and industry and commerce.

Naturally committees vary in size according to local conditions—in 1968 Luton's had 17 members and Lancashire's over 70—but generally they are large. This gives a clue to their function: they are more like the House of Commons than the Cabinet. The proceedings must be public and therefore open to the Press.

Yet much of their work is in fact done in private, in sub-committees. These sub-committees are not formed to avoid public discussion: they are needed because it would be impossible to transact all the many and varied items at one monthly meeting of a large body. Nevertheless it is convenient to be able to discuss certain matters—for instance, those involving an individual's personal affairs—in private. Other things may be only briefly discussed in a sub-committee but debated hotly in public when the Press are present.

The significance of the debate may be limited so far as voting is concerned, just as in Parliament. It is usual for members of the political parties to meet separately in advance of the committee to determine their collective attitude to major issues. Unlike Parliament there are co-opted members as well as elected ones on education committees : the intention is that they will broaden the base of discussion. Yet sometimes, by happy chance, 'persons of experience in education' co-opted by council members may share their political views. For that reason some would do away with the practice. Others talk of 'keeping politics out of education', a sentiment which may embody a noble ideal but which is wholly impractical. Education is after all a social and therefore a political question : public accountability demands control by those answerable to the electorate and in a developed society political parties are bound to form, and having formed, to organize the way their policy is put across.

The sub-committee is for most purposes the key unit in committee structure. The agenda for a monthly education committee meeting, chosen at random from one borough authority, includes over 300 items. They could not possibly all be discussed at one meeting especially by a large body : indeed on the face of it this is a formidable slab of work even for a group of sub-committees and it probably represents a greater-than-average control by members as distinct from officers.

The amount of delegation is the main factor in determining the amount of committee business and thus the number of sub-committees. The degree of delegation may in turn be largely the result of the amount of latitude allowed to the education committee by the council. The total situation reflects the size of the authority (for in a very big one it would be physically impossible not to delegate a good deal to officials) and also the kind of political atmosphere that exists in the area.

Paradoxically, striving after complete control of most issues may weaken the elected members' real influence. Of the 300 items on the agenda used as an example over 100 were acknowledged to be formal even at sub-committee level by inclusion in a separate part of the agenda. A similar number were items passed over in the sub-committees with a single word—'agreed'. The remainder, either items of importance or those that caught the attention of particular members, were discussed at greater length in sub-committees. All but six were approved by the full committee without debate.

It is at least arguable that delegation of all save 20 or 30 of the items to officials would have spot-lighted the important issues and allowed more time for them to be debated fully and with more careful preparation by the members. Nor is this argument merely a device by bureaucrats to seize more power, for it is sad but true that some officers prefer a system of little rather than great delegation. Official committee approval can absolve them from unpleasant decisions and from responsibility for their consequences; furthermore the greater the amount of material in front of a committee the simpler it is for an official to ease through projects dear to his heart.

But all education committees need some sub-division however much they delegate. An obvious one is between work concerned with schools and with further education. Within schools there may be a further split into primary, secondary and special education. Advantages and disadvantages are nicely balanced : separate consideration of problems peculiar to one sector and division of labour favour the split but as all sectors have much in common many items may be dealt with several times over.

There are similar possibilities in further education. Colleges of education and colleges of further education are (perhaps not very logically) usually taken together : as may be adult education, awards, youth and community services and youth employment. Adult education normally goes, as a sort of poor relation, with the colleges but most authorities have a separate youth committee, as recommended by the Albemarle Report. The Employment and Training Act 1948 requires participating authorities to set up youth employment committees with industrial representation but they may in practice be subordinated to the further education sub-committees. Awards committees are less frequent with increasing Government control. The choice between one sub-committee and five or six will depend not so much on the size of the authority, though this is relevant, as on the degree of delegation to officials and on the attitude to the various branches of the work by committee members.

Apart from the main types of institution the ancillary services may be put under a sub-committee. 'Special services' may include school health, school meals and school attendance and welfare (perhaps together with special schools). Alternatively, each may have a separate sub-committee. There may be another for sites and buildings, a complicated and costly branch of the work. Many committees have a finance sub-committee to keep a watch on the enthusiasms of the others.

Theoretical arguments may strongly favour separate sub-committees for as many branches as possible, but in practice there are grave defects in having too many. One is the sheer amount of time required to call, service and attend them all: if there is little actual business it may be inordinate. When regular meetings are held with little pressure of events the officers may have to struggle to get together an agenda at all. Provided the grouping of sub-divisions of the committee's work is logical there is little danger of neglecting any aspect from having too few sub-committees—and it is always easier to create them later than to reduce the number.

Whatever the system the time taken to give decisions is usually regarded as the acid test of a local education authority structure. There may be earlier stages in the operation—governors, divisional executives—and later ones, such as a finance sub-committee. It may then go to full education committee and finally the council itself. Each stage may have a different function and the ultimate decision may be the better for it, but it is arguable whether so many stages are ever necessary. They are certainly not *always* necessary: if every item is duplicated the process is slow and frustrating. Yet one of the difficulties about local government committees is their lack of selectivity. The machine tends to grind everything at the same speed and to the same size.

Lower-tier committees

County education committees have traditionally been less required to submit matters for consideration by finance committees and councils, but the 1944 Act provided for the bigger ones to delegate certain functions to committees at district level called divisional executives. Many districts had had education committees of their own before the Act and they wanted to continue to have some measure of local control.

Some 150 of these executives were set up, with the Minister acting as umpire in case a county and one of its districts disagreed about the need for sub-division. The degree of delegation was, apart from a few areas, extended only to primary and secondary education, with further education, except for evening institutes and youth and community work, remaining a county responsibility. Policy matters were not fully delegated—not for instance finance, or development plans; but rather the appointment of assistant teachers, and non-teaching staff, school holidays, tenancies of schools, attendance, school meals, grants to pupils and so on.

Forty-four towns with populations over 60,000 (or school populations over 7,000) were given rather more independence. In these Excepted Districts the Town Council, which became the divisional executive and set up its own Committee for Education, was empowered to spend within approved estimates and, subject to overall approval by the county, to draw up its own development plan.

Some have claimed for divisional executives greater local participation in decision-making and speedier decisions on delegated matters. Others including Sir William Alexander, the Secretary of the Association of Education Committees, have argued that this local participation only comes at the expense of removing powers from school or college governing bodies and that decision-making is slowed up by the presence of an extra layer.

Generalization is difficult because practice has varied so considerably, and because any system can be made to work given good elected members and good officers. The precise form local participation should take is unlikely ever to be resolved satisfactorily, but, particularly as authorities grow bigger, good administrators will agree that some form of it is essential if education is to remain alive and accessible to the people for whom it is intended. Experience shows, however, that more is involved than simply setting up another committee : sometimes this can have the opposite effect from what is intended.

Divisional education officers, or other district officers, are always likely to be necessary regardless of whether they serve a district committee or not. A strictly local point of reference for parents and schools can perhaps do more to make an education authority truly effective and responsive to public need than any amount of highly-polished administrative machinery at headquarters. District officers can also by their local knowledge and allegiance coupled with a professional knowledge of the way the education system works, give the best possible service to governors and managers of schools and colleges.

Governors and managers

(a) County schools

Primary schools have managers; secondary schools have governors who tend to have more power. This is an unsatisfactory distinction, but one that runs through the whole system. For county secondary schools the LEA makes an Instrument of Government : the size of the body and its representation varies but will often include university, church and industry as well as education committee or other local council members. There is often keen competition to serve though it may regrettably be followed by frustration. Often this stems from uncertainty about powers and duties which turn out to be rather less than some people suppose.

The powers are set out in Articles of Government which require ministerial approval and so are fairly standard throughout the country : but this leaves plenty of scope for variety of interpretation and practice. They include, for instance, preparation of annual financial estimates, a phrase that can be almost meaningless when the authority treats all schools according to a formula for staffing, books, stationery and materials. The governors may submit requirements in furniture and equipment, but these will be considered centrally and the sums allowed are more likely to depend on an administrative estimate of need modified by available finance than on the governors' requests. Governors normally appoint assistant teachers (and are represented at appointments of heads) and other staff. This tends to be their most substantial set of duties and is probably the one that gives them most satisfaction. The head of course is always present and, one hopes, very influential in making these appointments; there will also usually be a representative of the chief education officer.

Governors may also be responsible for the 'general direction of the conduct and curriculum of the school', responsibility bounded in practice by (*a*) the authority's responsibility for the general educational character of the school and its place in the local system and (*b*) the head's control of internal organization, management and discipline. If the Articles contain words of this kind as envisaged by the 1943 White Paper on Reconstruction, they are not very easy to interpret, and it may be that between the millstones of the authority and the head the governors' power may be somewhat compressed.

This kind of arrangement is in fact characteristic of much of the education system : guide lines are given rather than strict regulation, and theory is always substantially modified in practice. The division of responsibilities suggested in the White Paper is a corrective to the theory that the teacher is completely free in this country to devise his own curriculum. In fact 'teacher' in this context usually means 'head teacher', in itself a significant modification.

41

And in practice the head is only free to present whatever programme is acceptable to public opinion. In this instance the governors are an aspect of public opinion.

With such a variable and generalized basis it is not profitable to speak of 'the relationship' between governors, authorities and heads. It is in truth a series of relationships, temporary alliances and regroupings. Governors are perhaps most frequently in harness with heads, supporting their causes even in opposition to the LEA. Yet many of them are also members of the LEA and must have regard to the needs of an area as a whole which may conflict with those of a particular school. Then again the governors may discourage a head from some course of action. And sometimes the head and the education officer representing the authority will unite together to oppose the viewpoint of the governors.

The education officer himself plays more than one role. The job of clerk to the governors, which he usually performs, is not quite the same as representative of the authority at governors' meetings. Combination of the two jobs in one man is sensible since many matters go from governors to secondary education sub-committee, and many rulings come from sub-committee to governing bodies. Good communication is vital. But there are temptations which have to be resisted. If the governors take a line which the education officer will have to oppose at the sub-committee stage he must say so, not remain silent and shoot them down later.

In large authorities neither the chief education officer nor one of his senior administrative colleagues may attend governors' meetings. He may be represented by an adviser (or organizer or inspector, whatever the local term is) or by a junior administrator. The large number of governing bodies may make this inevitable. If so it is essential that his own lines of communication are good : his representatives must understand the policy and must take and bring back full information on important issues.

The chief education officer has other essential duties in this indistinct and uncertain realm. One is to try to clarify for all those concerned the role they have to play. New heads, governing bodies themselves and his own administrative and advisory staff should all be given a chance, through courses, conferences and written information, to form a picture of what is supposed to happen. The young administrator may find that one of his first jobs is to represent his chief at a governors' meeting. If the chief can go with him on this first occasion it will help : in any case he should have clear unambiguous instructions about his duties and his role.

One of the biggest difficulties arises from sheer weight of numbers. The presence of many separate governing bodies provides a tendency towards conflict with the one, unifying policy of the education committee. The more bodies there are the harder it is to find members of the right calibre and to keep everyone informed about their duties. Some authorities, particularly urban ones, solve the problem by having groups of governors and managers. Properly run group boards of this kind can still safeguard the interests of individual schools but also have a better chance of influencing the education committee through collective strength as well as reducing the number of points of contact between authority and local representatives to manageable proportions.

Grouping is more common for primary schools, partly reflecting the relatively small amount of business each school produces, and partly the normally lower status of managers' activities in the eyes of authorities. The Instrument of Management may apply to any number of schools and the Rules (not Articles) are not subject to the approval of the Secretary of State.

Whatever the pattern the nature of the membership will often largely determine the quality of the work that is done. To some extent this depends on the trouble education authorities take to ensure effective representation of the local community, but it hinges even more on the function governors and managers are supposed to perform. We shall return to this question in the final chapter.

(b) Voluntary schools

The gradual absorption of church schools into the state system has been marked by a series of compromises. The 1944 Act gave a choice to voluntary schools—more freedom, less financial help; more outside control, more financial support. The differences show themselves in the arrangements for the government and management of schools, for though the broad principles remain, of Instrument and Articles of Government (for secondary schools) and Instrument and Rules of Management (for primary schools), there are big differences from the county sector.

Voluntary *aided* schools still belong to the trustees and they are responsible for the upkeep of the outside of the premises : the education authority meets all other running costs, both for maintenance, equipment and teachers' salaries. The trustees get a grant direct from the Department of Education and Science of 80 per cent of the costs of new buildings, improvements and maintenance. Most aided schools are religious foundations, and in England are almost all Roman Catholic. Religious instruction is in accordance with the trust deed, two-thirds of the governors and managers are appointed by the trustees, the governors or managers can appoint all teachers including heads (provided the appointments are approved on educational grounds by the authority) and they are free to use the premises outside school hours unless they are needed for educational purposes.

There are about 5,000 aided compared with 19,000 county schools which is some evidence of the not ungenerous financial arrangements which confer quite tangible freedom. In other ways the schools are run much as the same as other local authority schools and the religious and educational authorities work together without friction. The division of responsibility for maintenance between the outside and the inside of the building entails a good deal of expertise in the offices of the education and the religious authorities and there is sometimes disagreement. But as in so much else, good personal relations overcome most problems.

In *controlled* schools, mainly sponsored by the Church of England and the free churches, the local authority meets the whole cost of running the schools and the foundation managers and governors amount to only one-third of the board. The authority is responsible for appointing staff, but the foundation managers can decide how the premises are used on Sundays and the whole board how they are used on Saturdays. If the trust deed specifies a particular kind of religious creed, the morning assembly is carried out according to its rules, but religious instruction is only denominational if the parents wish it. 'Reserved teachers' may be appointed for this purpose. With these relatively minor exceptions the schools operate very much like the county schools. There is a very small group of secondary schools (about 150) that falls mid-way between aided and controlled status, the *special agreement* school created as a result of the 1936 Education Act designed to help voluntary schools to expand. Here two-thirds of the board are foundation governors, and religious instruction is given in accordance with the trust deed, but apart from reserved teachers the staff are appointed by the LEA.

(c) *Further education*

The governing bodies of colleges of further education run by local education authorities are, in comparison with their primary and secondary counterparts, much more broadly based and much more powerful. The authority must set up a board of governors for a technical college, college of art, college of commerce, residential adult education college or farm institute, and the board must have substantial representation from industry and commerce and other interests, including universities and professional bodies where the college offers advanced courses. They usually have certain specific authority of a substantial kind delegated to them, such as the appointment of staff and the right to draw up their own financial estimates. Principals are usually appointed by a joint committee of the authority and the governors.

The work of these colleges is so diverse and so beyond the experience of most education committee members that they are usually glad to have the advice of industrialists and others about their needs, though the authority in appointing elected members from its own ranks expects them to try to control any wild extravagances, and, of course, incidentally to gain experience of the world of further education. Finance has become an increasing source of disagreement with college governors as the costs of further education and the amount of provision have grown enormously in recent years. Yet authorities are generally glad to spend whatever they can on these institutions and they can be very proud of their record in creating the basis on which modern technology stands : technical education in this country is very much the product of local initiative and local pride.

But rapid growth has led to overlap and in recent years pressure has mounted nationally and locally for rationalization; that is, closing courses with small numbers and transferring others to larger colleges. Again this can lead to disagreement with college governors and principals whose concern is with building up their own college. The consultative and regulatory processes of further education are many and complex, however, and they will be discussed in a later section. At this stage one other brief reference should be made. The recently created polytechnics have been given a freedom from local authority control that goes well beyond normal arrangements : the governors have control of the running of these colleges within the annual sum agreed for their running costs, leaving the authority to determine the general character of the college and to fix the level of fees and approve capital expenditure. It is no exaggeration to say that this is greater freedom than most education committees allow their own sub-committees and greater than some councils allow their education committees. It is an interesting innovation, designed to retain important institutions within the local government financial structure without curtailing their freedom. Only time will tell how it will work, but its importance could extend beyond the confines of further education and could lead to an examination of the essential freedoms required by the education service as a whole.

Similar arrangements have been introduced for the government of LEA colleges of education, already freed from most of the financial restrictions of local government by the pooling arrangements. The Robbins Report recommended their removal from local control and inclusion within the university sector as recognition of their increasing status as educational establishments and the need to improve still further their academic level. The Government, recognizing the vital importance of these establishments to the local education authorities as a source of teacher supply and, we may hope, the highly successful way the authorities have built them up, sought ways of improving links with universities without completely removing that with the local authority.

The government of the remaining further education establishments is largely a matter of local discretion. Section 43 of the 1944 Act gave the Secretary of State power to make regulations for establishing county colleges, for compulsory part-time education of young people up to the age of 18. No regulations have been issued and the idea may now be presumed dead. One or two authorities have set up county colleges on a voluntary basis and they are run like other colleges of further education, though they concentrate mainly on non-vocational courses. The Crowther Report recommended that of two unfulfilled provisions of the Act, the raising of the school leaving age to 16 and the county colleges, priority should be given to the first.

Residential colleges of adult education, though few in number, are successfully run by a number of authorities, sometimes jointly with neighbours or financially aided by them. The government of these colleges, concerned mainly with short courses for adults in pursuit of culture or business firms and trades unions seeking enlightenment on management problems, is one of the pleasanter tasks in educational administration. Youth clubs and community centres run by LEAs are normally given a management committee with the usual mixture of authority and voluntary members. These less orthodox sectors of the service do not readily respond to the conventional pattern and it has to be recorded that although things have improved in recent years there is still room for a more imaginative approach : this will be discussed in a later chapter.

Regional co-ordination

Further education

Until 1944 further education was a power, not a duty, of local education authorities. The Act took a step forward with the idea of a progressive three-stage system culminating in further education but it only scratched the surface of the problem of creating a coherent national system. The Percy Report of 1945 spelt it out with great clarity. Industry it said required 'a responsive and adaptable organization for technological education. The existing provision for such education lacks focus. Not only is it divided between Universities and Technical Colleges but each university and college tends to act independently.' The report recommended among other things 'Regional Advisory Councils, similar to some already existing, should be set up for all areas of England and Wales and they should co-ordinate technological studies in universities and technical colleges'. Ten councils were set up in 1947 and they have continued ever since, occupying an uncertain and to some extent unenviable role in the national pattern, but in view of all the difficulties achieving reasonable success.

Sir Peter Venables pointed out, a little unkindly, one of their troubles: 'Some are representation run riot, with everything but the kitchen stove.' The usual pattern with representation from every authority and every college, universities and major industry in the region makes the Regional Councils themselves unfitted for anything except formal approval of sub-committee work and occasional letting off steam from the disaffected. Everything depends on the sub-committees and here again there are problems. One is the uncertain status of the council. Any Regional body has a role as yet inadequately defined in our administrative and legislative pattern. And like every other body that is Advisory those affected by its views tend to want to accept advice favourable to them and reject the rest.

There are built-in tensions, sometimes between the college principals themselves when one's expansion tends to be at another's expense, and sometimes between authorities as a result. At other times the principals as a body may see their interest in general expansion threatened by the collective interest of the authorities in rationalization. Specialisms conflict with general organizational needs; industry may find the academic and administrative worlds insensitive to their needs whereas the providers of technical education may often wish that industry had a clearer idea of its own requirements.

General direction and control of the Council may be in the hands of a fairly small steering committee (under different names). This will have a majority of local authority representatives for they find the money for the venture : often these will be education officers rather than elected members who tend to serve mainly on the Council itself. There will also be an Academic Board, with a majority of college principals concerned with the general pattern of provision for the various industries and a number of Advisory Committees, mainly of teachers and industrialists, to advise on the needs of their own specialisms. Other committees may deal with training courses for teachers, liaison with schools and perhaps problems peculiar to the individual regions. Every region is likely to have one very important committee concerned with the control and approval of advanced courses, and it is with this activity mainly in a negative context that most people in further education associate the Regional Councils.

The approval of the Secretary of State is required before courses roughly above the standard of GCE 'A' level are provided in colleges of further education. This approval is usually given by the Regional Staff Inspector (a senior HMI) and applications are submitted through Regional Advisory Councils. The normal practice is for the RSI to join with the appropriate sub-committee (mainly chief education officers or their further education officers) to discuss each application and reach a decision which although ultimately that of the Inspector is in practice never taken without full consultation and almost invariably agreement.

Authorities are required to consult their neighbours in fixing the fees they charge for further education courses and the Regional Advisory Council is sometimes, though not always, the medium chosen for these consultations. Similarly such matters as the salaries paid to part-time teachers and the arrangements for reimbursement of charges for the education of students from other authorities' areas may be decided in the Regional Council though as we shall see there are other ways of doing this.

General

Local education committees find the need to co-operate on a whole variety of things. They may do this on a very local, *ad hoc* basis or they may do it through a regional association of education committees. The usual pattern is that each authority is represented by either officers or members or both and that occasional meetings of the full body provide a sounding board for opinion. In between, however, working parties of officers consider specific matters referred to them and report it to the parent body. None of the decisions are binding on member authorities but they are a useful way of exchanging information, and particularly, of bringing policies into line where variations might adversely affect the public.

Some of the topics discussed by one such association recently include:

Payment of travelling expenses and subsistence allowances
to teachers attending local teachers' centres;
Inter-Authority Payments for No-Area Students;
Recreational Facilities;
Income Scales for the provision of necessitous and
distinctive clothing;
Scales of Assistance for Boarding Education;
Full-time Integrated Industrial Training Courses;
Ordinary Level Fees for General Certificate of Education;
Further Education Awards;
Payment of Teachers for Invigilation Duties;
Schools Museum Service;
Management Committees of Curriculum Development Centres;
Further Education—Grading of Courses;
Intermediate Awards for Further Education Students.

An interesting example of regional co-operation is in the world of examinations. Regional examination unions for technical education have existed since the nineteenth century when the Union of Lancashire and Cheshire Institutes and the Union of Educational Institutions were formed. They and others still honourably continue, in association with the City & Guilds of London, to provide regional variations on the national pattern to meet distinctively local needs. The familiar system is used of a large parent body comprised of local authorities, teachers and industry, served by sub-committees, mainly of teachers in this case. Regional co-operation on what is still the main examination for schools, is, however, much looser. The General Certificate of Education is administered by eight *ad hoc* examination boards strongly influenced by the universities and having small links with local education authorities. On the other hand, the Certificate of Secondary Education, aimed specifically at less academic pupils but likely in time to replace the Ordinary level of the GCE in all schools, is much more broadly based and centred firmly on the schools and the local authorities. Teachers and education officers from the participating authorities form the Board itself, and sub-committees, for examinations, dominated by teachers, and for finance, with the officers more strongly in evidence, deal with policy. There are of course controlling advisory committees of teachers for every subject examined.

National co-ordination

Local education authorities must co-operate nationally as well as regionally not only to co-ordinate their policies but to negotiate with their main partners, the Secretary of State and the teachers' associations. Local authorities, except London (which has traditionally been considered big enough to represent itself) belong to either the County Councils Association or the Association of Municipal Corporations. The importance and special features of education are recognized by the existence of a third body, the Association of Education Committees. The relationship between the AEC and the other two bodies is very similar to that between an education committee and its council : strictly speaking the CCA and the AMC, which incidentally have Education Committees of their own, have all the authority and the AEC has none, but in practice the AEC and its Secretary, Sir William Alexander, exercise very great influence.

On major matters concerning education the three associations march together. For instance, each is represented on the various Burnham Committees : on the main panel the CCA has 9 members, the AMC and the AEC six each. Similarly each is consulted by the Department of Education and Science before new circulars and regulations are issued. The associations, through their executive committees, negotiate in the interests of their members and are able to influence the course of events, for example by suggesting amendments to the draft documents. The AEC is naturally the one with which education officers and their committees are most familiar (though it must be stressed that they are strongly represented in all relevant branches of the work of the CCA and AMC) and its relationship with its members has been described by its Secretary as fourfold.

First, the secretariat itself is available throughout the year to give advice on any matters within the jurisdiction of an education committee. Second, the AEC negotiates with the teachers' associations to resolve common problems. Third, the AEC is an instrument of day-to-day negotiation with the Department of Education and Science on behalf of members. Fourth, the AEC represents its members on over eighty national bodies or advisory committees that are involved with education in some way or other.

To refer to each or even most of these bodies would be tedious : most of them can be found, together with a lot of other information, in the Education Committees Year Book. Some of them, however, can be briefly mentioned. In further education there is the National Advisory Council on Education for Industry and Commerce, from which sub-committees are set up to report on particular aspects of education : this is the national counterpart of the Regional Advisory Councils, though of course its functions are different. The Association of Technical Institutions is a loose federation of technical colleges and local authorities, meeting in the regions and twice yearly nationally, to confer on current educational issues. The Association of Art Institutions has a similar role in its own sphere. A different function is performed by the Council for National Academic Awards, an autonomous body with power to award degrees and similar qualifications to students in technical colleges. This body has even more importance than its title suggests, for by its preliminary advisory visits to colleges wishing to offer courses it suggests necessary standards of equipment, accommodation and staffing that strongly influence the character of technical colleges. The National Institute of Adult Education offers an advisory service and a medium of consultation for local education authorities, the WEA, university extra-mural departments and the many voluntary bodies concerned with adult education.

Outside traditional further education two bodies may be mentioned. The Central Training Council was set up under the Industrial Training Act 1964 to co-ordinate the activities of Industrial Training Boards for each major industry. The Board's duties are to provide training facilities for all employees; they can impose a levy on employers and give grants to those who provide approved training. Education authorities through their technical colleges assist with this provision and they are represented on the Central Training Council and on the various Boards. The National Youth Employment Council, which advises the Secretary of State in the administration of the Employment & Training Act 1948 also has representatives of education authorities.

A most important national committee on the schools' side is the Schools Council which was set up in 1964 to keep under review the curriculum, teaching methods and examinations in primary and secondary schools. This is a most significant development in view of the traditional attitude of individual enterprise in these matters. Teachers, together with Her Majesty's Inspectors and education officers, are for the first time attempting to organize research, articulate their own views on the best teaching methods, and initiate experiment. There are many sub-committees : one to co-ordinate the use of staff and finance in research projects; one to co-ordinate the work of the regional CSE Boards; another for the GCE; and ten subject panels.

The 1944 Act created two Central Advisory Councils for Education, one for England, one for Wales, with the duty of advising the Secretary of State on educational theory and practice. After a slow start the Councils with a series of important reports— Crowther, Newsom and Plowden—have begun to exercise great influence on the educational life of the country, though their recommendations have by no means all found favour with the Governments to whom they have reported. As at many other points in our system influence rather than legal force is the way that changes tend to come.

Finally the many professional associations in the education service play their part in shaping the course of events. The teachers' organizations and notably those represented on the various Burnham Committees are tremendously influential, and not merely in negotiating salaries and conditions of service, though this is an important influence on the service. Policy statements on major educational issues, local and regional branches to pool resources and discuss common problems, discussion and negotiation with the Secretary of State and with their employers, the local authorities, both nationally and locally—these are the regular ways in which the teaching profession makes its mark on the pattern of events The National Union of Teachers, the National Association of Schoolmasters, the Joint Four, the National Association of Head Teachers, the Association of Principals and of Teachers in Technical Institutions, the Association of Teachers in Colleges and Departments of Education are familiar, particularly through their initials, to everyone involved in education. Apart from teachers there is an association of inspectors and organizers, the National Association of Inspectors and Educational Organizers; one for Youth Employment Officers, the Institute of Youth Employment Officers; and one for Youth Service Officers, the National Association of Youth Service Officers, each in their own sphere making a contribution both educationally and in raising professional standing. Administrators have their own associations, at present about to amalgamate as the Society of Education Officers. The Association of Chief Education Officers operate at national level, but the Association of Education Officers, which included in its membership as well as chief officers, deputy and assistant chief officers and divisional education officers, has for many years had regional branches where members meet regularly to discuss educational and administrative matters within their own circle—in fact, to talk shop, which is what all good education officers like to do better than anything else in the world.

4

Inside the
education office

It is time to come out of the committee room and go into the office. A local education authority is required by law to appoint a Chief Education Officer and the Secretary of State must be satisfied that he is a fit person for the post. No indication is given of the qualifications required but it is the general practice for appointments to be made from people with a good degree and teaching and administrative experience, normally in an education office. In the early post-war days it was not unusual for chief education officers to have had very little administrative experience on appointment : indeed there were relatively few subordinate educational administrative posts in which they could get their experience. Nowadays every office tends to have its own hierarchy and the aspirant must clamber his way up the ladder rung by rung.

The name 'Chief Education Officer' is a generic term, and although it is the one most frequently used there are variations. 'Director of Education' was at one time the standard usage but although it still exists many authorities have preferred to indicate a change of emphasis by changing the title. Other variations include 'County Education Officer', just plain 'Education Officer' (as in the ILEA) and 'Secretary for Education'. There is no difference in status or function. However, 'Borough Education Officer' usually means the principal officer of an Excepted District. 'Divisional Education Officer' is self-explanatory.

There is just as much variety in the titles of subordinate professional officers in Education Departments, and sometimes the same title may mean different things in different places. The confusion is increased by the fact that subordinate officers in large authorities may have higher salaries than chief officers in smaller ones.

At the second-tier level of authority the key word is usually 'Deputy': it may be 'Deputy Chief Education Officer' or 'Deputy Education Officer' or 'Deputy Director of Education'. At the third-tier the word is 'Assistant'—usually 'Assistant Education Officer' or 'Assistant Director'. 'Senior Assistant Education Officer' may mean the senior third-tier officer but it may mean that there is a fourth tier known as 'Assistant Education Officer'. Usually, however, the fourth-tier officer is known as an 'Administrative Assistant' (though here again he may be called 'Senior Administrative Assistant' or even, in at least one authority, 'Education Officer'). In this book the terms used are Chief Education Officer (or CEO), Deputy Education Officer (or Deputy), Assistant Education Officer (or AEO) and Administrative Assistant. Perhaps these are as near to a norm as it is possible to get. Collectively the term used will be education officers.

As names, so functions: the ways of sub-dividing the work of education departments are almost equally various. It is no use describing a model organization when so much depends on particular local circumstances. History plays its part in most offices and there are very great variations in size.

The next chapter will consider some of the principles and problems of departmental organization, but first we need to look at the content of the work. For this an arbitrary division into four branches is assumed: primary and secondary education; special services; further education; sites and buildings. The newcomer to administration from teaching may well find himself an administrative assistant in one of these branches or even, in small authorities, in charge of one.

Primary and secondary education

The officer responsible for the administration of primary education has to deal with more children, more teachers and more buildings than any other branch. His clients include some of the nicest people in the whole service working in some of the worst conditions. They have to manage with the lowest *per capita* budget for books, stationery, materials and equipment. The primary schools have been the pioneers of educational advance and they have done it in spite of steady neglect.

It is accepted, in educational psychology and in common

experience, that the early years are important to a child. Yet pro-
portionately very much more of our resources have gone on
secondary and further education. There has been a built-in assumption in most aspects of administration that more should be spent
on older pupils. Of course, the more elaborate equipment needed
for more advanced work and the greater cost of, say, sixth form
text books are legitimate weightings. It is inevitable, if unfortunate,
that teachers' salary scales should reflect the need to attract those
more highly qualified academically for secondary and further education (though it may have been overdone).

Yet how are we to explain the assumption that primary schools
can manage with bigger classes than secondary? It is at least partly
the fact that the greater primary school population needs propor-
tionately more money to achieve improvements; partly, too, because
defects, such as behaviour or learning problems, only become conspicuous later on. For these children we have concentrated on
attempted cure rather than prevention. The system favours those
likely to succeed rather than those likely to need help.

The primary education officer now at least has the Plowden
Report to help him make a case for higher standards in the years
when the child's future is being settled. Much of his attention may
be given to establishing which areas are in greatest need of educational compensation for inadequate home conditions. Special
building programmes may be allowed; above-scale allowances may
be allocated to teachers in schools in the worst areas. For all these
he will need to test the validity of a whole range of possible criteria
for assessing priorities and then make recommendations to the committee.

The basic organization of primary schools is into infant (five to
seven) and juniors (seven to eleven). Unless very small numbers are
involved they are likely to be separate, giving the advantage of a
headmistress with specialist knowledge of infants' work, but perhaps
certain disadvantages. Small separate infant schools increase the
number of head teachers required and some would prefer a smaller
number of (better-paid) heads. However, heads of junior mixed and
infant schools tend to be men who may be less attuned to the needs
of the vital earliest years. On the other hand for the less able pupils
the continuity of a single school might be preferable.

These matters will not be settled as theoretical exercises. Many
primary schools are likely to be voluntary and the religious authorities will have their views: existing buildings and existing traditions
will be influential, and so will the attitudes of the teachers' associa-

tions and of managing bodies. This relatively simple issue demonstrates in fact just how little academic theories of decision-making can be applied to education. The educational advantages and disadvantages are balanced; practical and management considerations are not straightforward; there are many special interests to be taken into account; decisions have to be reached democratically.

Whatever the organization the schools have to be staffed. Publicity campaigns to attract new teachers from college and to persuade married women to return to teaching have figured largely in the primary education officer's work. The number of full-time teachers that can be employed is controlled by a quota fixed annually by the Department of Education and Science: part-timers and returning married women have been needed to keep primary schools at even the low standards accepted as the target. Local financial resources have latterly assumed more importance than the quota, however, and an improvement in the supply of teachers—and therefore the quotas—has coincided with a period of economic stringency. Manpower planning in education is hazardous, locally as well as nationally.

The actual appointment is not normally the administrator's job: appointing probationers coming from college may fall to him or to an adviser but more senior jobs involving competition will be the responsibility of the managers or the education committee. He is intimately concerned, however, with fitting square pegs into the right-shaped holes in considering where new teachers are to begin their careers and with advising elected committees on choosing the right headmasters and headmistresses. This is his most qualitative function, and he will do well to remember it.

The primary education officer has some influence on the destiny of children, too. He controls, within the authority's general policy, their first admission to a school. In urban areas when certain schools are more popular than others he may have to fix admission zones; and he may have to decide whether any can be admitted before they are five. All the educational arguments favour individual consideration of whether the start should be early or later, part-time of full-time, with priority to those from homes least able to contribute much of value to the child's readiness for school. Harsh economic fact requires general rules, such as qualifying ages of entry and full-time or nothing.

Sadly, the administrator is more familiar with children in quantity than as individuals. At the primary stage forecasting the likely school population at various ages is a vital pre-requisite of building plans. Schools have to be planned several years in advance of use with their inclusion by the DES in a building programme as the mid-point of the exercise, between determining and justifying need and physical planning of the premises. First at administrative level, then at committee stage, the local priorities must be assessed and argued out. For primary schools for many years 'roofs over heads' has been the criterion with rare opportunity for replacing worn-out buildings. Since the Plowden Report this type of primary school has a better chance of inclusion in national building programmes. As they exist mainly in the centres of towns the problem of finding a site is an added difficulty, but at least there is more opportunity for remodelling existing premises. For the most part, though, movement of population, housing estates and overspill are likely to be the basic vocabulary in primary school building.

Long-term planning is needed, but it cannot be too long. Eight to ten years is probably the maximum: anything longer needs a crystal ball not a forecast and even this period may see frequent revisions. Planners and housing officers can usually provide at this range a reasonably approximate estimate of eventual child-population, through 'house-child product' for particular types of housing or a general forecast of the likely proportion of children per thousand population based on past experience, checked against actual birth rates as they become known.

Armed with this information the next objective is securing a building programme place in response to one of the Department's annual requests for submissions. The other side of planning, the physical lay-out of the school, will probably have to start in advance of approval. If the authority has a separate sites and buildings branch, responsibility may change hands at this point, though the primary education officer will want to play his part in ensuring that educational needs shape the building.

Indeed with good administration educational needs will shape the whole pattern of physical provision. Curriculum development is as much a live issue in education offices as in the schools. Administrators have played a leading part in establishing development centres, teachers' workshops for trying out new ideas, and in setting up machinery—development teams, conferences, steering committees—for formulating new thinking. But the most interesting aspect of the inter-play of administrative and educational ideas is the impact of curriculum development on new school planning: through it the traditional age division between primary and secondary has been challenged and new schools are appearing which embody this thinking. The middle school for children from eight or nine to twelve or thirteen is the result of initiative from one or two enlightened LEAs and their chief officers. Along with the middle school goes the notion of a four year first school to replace the present infant school : this would give continuity in the early years and also help avoid some of the problems of recruitment to headship referred to earlier.

The word 'Plowden' is likely to be heard frequently in this branch of the office. Perhaps in future emphasis on nursery education will turn out to be the most valuable legacy from this report. Government prohibition because of teacher-shortage for most of the post-war years has meant few places in nursery schools or classes. The position is changing at least in the cities because of the national urban programmes offering 75 per cent capital grants and similar support, at least temporarily, for running costs of new ventures in the social services in those areas in greatest need. Nursery schools have been emphasized and are increasingly being considered as ways of giving early educational support for socially disadvantaged children.

With this recent emphasis secondary education has begun to feel slightly cooler winds than it has enjoyed in the past. The changed balance of training in the colleges of education has produced more primary school teachers. Since most of them are women the wastage because of early marriage is high, but there has also been a net gain. Overall quotas of teachers for each authority are fixed by the DES and expansion in primary has meant marking-time for the secondary schools.

Comparatively, however, the secondary sector has been well staffed and until the impact of raising the school leaving age is felt the problem is rarely a question of recruiting numbers but of specialists in certain subjects. In both primary and secondary schools the number and nature of above-scale allowances for teachers is an important policy issue, on which the Burnham reports leave considerable discretion to the LEA. In both sectors, but particularly in secondary where the allowances and the complexities of organization are greater, there is considerable scope for the education officer to devise imaginative and flexible schemes that will allow discretion to heads to deploy their resources but at the same time ensure that the needs of the authority's children as a whole are being well served.

The kind of scheme that has most occupied secondary administrators in recent years, however, is that concerned with comprehensive reorganization. Most people have an idea of the political struggles and the educational issues and their legal implications that attach to this subject. Only those actually in the business can begin to realize how much administrative time and effort has gone into planning, reappraising, investigating, negotiating and afterwards implementing schemes. The reorganization exercise itself will be examined in a later chapter, but its implications affect much of the work of the secondary branch.

It has certainly affected one aspect, transfer from primary school, whether actual reorganization has taken place or not. The very terminology is significant for not long ago it would have seemed quite proper to talk about selection for secondary education, and the potential administrator in this branch had to steep himself in selection techniques. Few authorities still retain out-and-out selection by testing and much greater reliance is placed on the judgement of primary school heads. Methods of scaling these assessments can be just as complicated as the old 11+ examination and of course this approach lacks the administrative simplicity of the formal, apparently factually-based system. This is a small but tangible example of the way administration, by adapting itself to human needs, has become a subtler and so more difficult art.

Even if an authority has nothing but comprehensive schools, allocation to particular schools may not be easy. Some schools are likely to be more attractive than others and some way has to be found of filling them all and satisfying as far as possible parents' wishes. The pure doctrine of neighbourhood schools, though it is relatively easy to administer, has its drawbacks, for there are neighbourhoods and neighbourhoods and to concentrate all the children from under-privileged homes in one district at the same school can produce as great inequality of opportunity as segregation into selective and modern schools. On the other hand artificial methods of controlling admission by, say, fixing proportions of children of different intellectual standards, can take away much of the value of the comprehensive idea.

A further refinement of the difficulty occurs when the authority's schools are partly reorganized and comprehensive and selective schools must somehow co-exist. Is it possible, or fair, in an urban area to restrict admission according to where people live? Alternatively, if selection tests are held first to cream off the brightest children there can be no comprehensive schools. In at least one authority parents were asked to choose initially between a comprehensive school without any selection tests or the opportunity of competing for a selective school place. The sting in the tail for the second category was that the alternative was a secondary modern school. Though this is as fair a system as any, perhaps, it has its obvious drawbacks. This is a problem without solutions—only palliatives.

Administrators are concerned not only with new ideas but with their aftermath. Where large schools are created they have to try to anticipate and lessen possible difficulties. The fear that institutions of this size might neglect individual differences and needs led to new, flexible schemes of above-scale allowances to make it possible to appoint senior teachers with social responsibilities within the schools. From the creation of these posts there has been much to learn : the creation in itself is not enough if the people in them are not well-chosen, carefully briefed, if possible trained, properly used and given time away from teaching duties to do the job required. Similar administrative posts in schools need the same pre-conditions for success. Thus one of the by-products of reorganization has been the beginnings of intensive study of the workings of schools as institutions.

Management theory is for the first time being seen as applicable to running a school. The need for well-thought-out and extended systems of communications; problems of delegation and personal relationships; the impact of time-tabling on the disposition of staff and the use of resources generally—these are the themes of innumerable conferences and seminars. It is a field in which education officers can be of direct help to the schools and it may be that the inter-relationship of education and its administration will be still further strengthened by co-operative study of the schools' management problems and their solution.

The use of resources in its wider context has long been a cause for concern in secondary administration. Many education officers have seen it their duty to encourage sixth form development within every school : the flower of English education has been urged to grow wherever the soil looked remotely suitable. Others have tried to plan this growth : they have pointed out that uneconomic units are usually educationally dubious, too (from lack of the stimulation of a reasonably sized group for individual pupils), and that sixth forms in smaller schools unduly limit the choice of subjects from sheer lack of a range of specialist staff. With an extended range of entry in terms of ability comprehensive schools need sixth form courses other than the academic : an academic sixth form of any size will normally only grow from a very big comprehensive school. Most people associate the sixth form college idea with the Croydon authority who publicized the notion in the 1950s without actually implementing it. No education officer is likely to become wildly popular with heads of secondary schools for pursuing this notion but it may be that the first small beginnings of experiments now in hand will eventually prove the case.

If there were an education dictator intent on providing maximum effective choice to the student at minimum cost he might well start his enquiries here, including in them a hard look at the overlapping provisions in colleges of further education in many areas. The secondary education officer will find himself less titanically cast, perhaps arranging co-operative schemes between schools to share sixth form studies, selectively planning specialist accommodation and therefore future courses, in new schools, arranging day-release schemes for school children to attend technical college to use scarce facilities.

Within the framework of the best use of resources the administrator may see his job as helping to shift the orientation of secondary education from achieving externally set targets to meeting the divergent needs of young adults. At the academic end of the scale the demands of the universities and the influence of their admission requirements on GCE 'A' level and thus on the sixth forms has been little challenged by either schools or administrators. The best hope for change seems at present to come from within the universities. It is significant that administrators and committees do not, in this country, seek to establish principles, curricula and methods for teaching at this level. The Schools Council's work will be influential, no doubt, but desire for change has hitherto been expressed as a need for a new kind of institution that would (*a*) through its broader approach relate itself to technical colleges, industry, the social services as well as university admission and (*b*) through its strength in concentrating resources be powerful enough to make its influence felt.

Similarly the creation of the Certificate in Secondary Education has set up an administrative device through which teachers can shape examinations from the educational needs of the children. The new must grow up alongside the old, first challenge it and then perhaps replace it. Meanwhile smaller but insistent questions need to be answered. Should children be entered for GCE as well as CSE? Should the authority pay for this? Which GCE examining board should be used and why? Is there any longer a need for sub-GCE examinations designed by the further education examining bodies?

It is interesting, too, that so far it is an examination, the CSE, that seems most likely to influence secondary education for the average pupil in the direction suggested by the Newsom Report. 'Bringing in the outside world' may continue to smack of sky-larking around, filling up the time of non-academic and therefore problem children, to many teachers and committee members, unless it can be shown through an imaginative examining technique that these things really are valuable.

The next really dramatic change will come when the school leaving age is raised to sixteen in 1972-3. Future historians will no doubt record whether the proposal's postponement in 1968 was due entirely to economic crisis or to its failure to capture public and professional imagination. The impact of keeping at school young adults, perhaps reluctant and probably uninterested in traditional approaches, will be tremendous, quite apart from the extra demands on teachers and buildings.

Special services

Most offices have a branch concerned with detecting and helping those with special needs. This side of educational administration has had less limelight than the large-scale dramatic tensions of the other branches. A great deal of unspectacular progress has been made particularly in providing schools for handicapped children and there are great opportunities for advance in the future. With national review of the social services generally there is a need for education authorities to clarify their objectives. There is uncertainty of purpose throughout the education service, but nowhere is it more damaging than in 'special services' work.

What does it mean? The administrator who applies for jobs in this branch will find it means something different in almost every authority. It may or may not include special schools; it may be concerned with various welfare services, perhaps including school meals. The school health service may or may not be a part. The differences reflect the confusion about objectives and the terminology by now has come to undervalue the services concerned: the connotations of 'special' and the overtones of 'welfare' are a hindrance to progress.

Arbitrary definition is necessary as a basis for discussion: it will reflect a personal point of view. The purpose, then, is to discover any factors, social, intellectual, physical or emotional that may prevent an individual child from benefiting from education in a primary or secondary school; to give advice and render help to the child and its family; to provide special education or other treatment to those discovered to be in need; and to co-operate with other agencies, statutory and voluntary, engaged in related work. Three separate but connected sectors of work are concerned: the school health service; special schools; and school attendance and welfare.

The administrator in charge will be very fortunate if he has a united command. The Medical Officer of Health may act as Principal School Medical Officer which makes sense economically and also logically for he has responsibilities for people before they go to school and again after they have left. On the other hand in a large authority there is little economic advantage, for a full-time separate staff is needed for the schools and co-operation is immeasurably easier if the senior school medical officer is on the CEO's staff. Either way without close links much of the potential of the service will be unrealized.

Even the more obviously medical aspects of the school health service—medical inspection, dental inspection and treatment—can be troublesome without good co-operation with the teacher with the aim of interfering as little as possible with the work of the schools. Medical records can be vitally helpful to teachers in seeing their pupils as individuals and the school nurse can often play an important part through knowledge of home backgrounds: conversely the teachers' knowledge can be invaluable to the doctors. Within the psychological aspects of school health there is an equal need for co-operation and its two-way nature is even more essential. Child guidance clinics for emotionally disturbed children can make little progress if the psychologists, social workers and psychiatrists work in isolation from the schools. It may be difficult to separate an emotional from an intellectual problem when it arises in a school and the psychologist can help teachers to look beyond superficial causes of backwardness. On the other hand there appear to teachers to be some problems which are straightforward educational ones and they see disadvantages in obscuring these issues, perhaps losing precious time on the way. Some authorities have separate schools psychological services within the education service for this type of problem. Any situation is a balance of advantages but here there seems an avoidable complication. Separate bands of experts sorting out potential clients from the same source, particularly if each is administratively responsible to a separate department, would seem to demand liaison of a high order and the dual approach does not on the face of it look the best way of discovering a child's difficulty. Even within this one sector of special services the complications are immense and the education officer will need much patience and skill to fashion a team approach.

Special schools, though educational establishments educationally run, rely heavily on the school health service for diagnosis of handicap in potential pupils and for subsequent treatment. The range of handicaps—from the basically physical to the basically educational —the gradations within that range, the inter-action of physical and educational factors, and the growing numbers now surviving with shattering and hitherto fatal handicaps, often multiple, show again how hard it is to deal with 'educational' problems on their own. Inter-authority co-operation, to make use of limited resources, and the continued existence of voluntary agencies offering residential special education add new dimensions to the needs for liaison. And not a few of the children in special schools may have other, social, problems too.

This may be especially true in the largest category, for the educationally sub-normal. There is another fundamental and very human difficulty. Parents are almost always reluctant to contemplate the need for this kind of treatment : to point out that it carries no social stigma is insufficient, and the fact that there is inevitably a subjective element in the assessment of intellectual sub-normality makes matters worse. Appeals to the DES against ascertainment are understandable but the consequent delay in securing special treatment may be harmful to the child.

One real difficulty is in the lack of common agreement about the level of attainment below which education in a separate school is justified. Authorities who can provide small remedial units within the normal school provision are perhaps better placed, though this is more difficult to achieve at the primary school level where treatment is most likely to achieve lasting results. Physical planning problems are thus overlaid with philosophical questions even greater than those in other schools : accurate and adequate medical records and advance information are not enough. The energetic pursuit of the traditional aims of successful educational administration, establishing the widest possible range of institutions, is not necessarily the best approach here. The concern is more with individual needs, an infinite gradation of them, and the human needs of handicapped children are likely to be best served by emphasizing their normality rather than their handicap. The other side of the coin is securing public acceptance of differences and needs as an aspect of life rather than as occasions for pity or charity.

The dramatic advances made in educating special school children have had less publicity than the leap forward in medical science that has ensured survival for so many more acutely handicapped. Significantly the main spring of action can be related to the emergence of a tangible, recognizable goal: it is in essence no different from the aim of many ordinary schools, but paradoxically the severity of the disability seems to carry in itself a more vivid illustration of the paramount need. Most special schools have in their sights the aim of making their pupils self-reliant, dependable, able to achieve a satisfactory marriage and to run a home. The re-examination of the curriculum freed from the assumptions and traditions of conventional schools has enabled special school teachers to make a significant contribution to educational thought generally. Some schools, notably those for maladjusted children, have pointed the way to progress through careful study of the influence of environment, notably home background, and have successfully sought to supply a stable framework in which children can reasonably be expected to begin to adjust themselves.

When individual attention is so important, good staff selection is vital. The most careful assessment of the needs of the job and of the attitudes of the applicant will pay dividends more than in any other branch of the service. It is a curious fact that governing bodies have only recently been set up for special schools, though these schools more than others need support and interest from men and women who can strengthen the links with the local community. These links, and close contacts with primary and secondary schools, will be one of the main contributions the administrator can make to developing special education still further.

The third element of this hypothetical special services branch is school attendance and welfare. The name may vary and so may the functions, but this one illustrates the two elements that predominate in this invaluable branch of the office. The education welfare officer, translated from school attendance officer, has himself undergone a significant change since his origins after 1870 when school boards were empowered to appoint officers to enforce their bye-laws on attendance. Since 1902 LEAs have been given many extra, related duties including regulation of the employment of children and the provision of clothing to allow children to go to school: the change of name incorporates the growing welfare function such as reporting suspected cases of handicap for investigation by medical officers and advising on home backgrounds of children appearing in the juvenile courts. The welfare officer's function of visiting homes puts him in a very special position and he is an essential link between home, school and officialdom.

Yet his status is ambivalent and will remain so as long as school attendance is a matter of law enforcement. Most people agree that some ultimate sanction is needed but experience of the formal processes satisfies no one. A sanction is a clumsy instrument of policy and most enlightened school attendance committees see the importance of getting beyond the facts of absence and legal obligation to try to detect trouble at the incipient stage. Fines cannot eradicate social sickness. Unfortunately the machinery for dealing with the broader aspects of attendance problems is rickety in the extreme. There are plenty of wheels but nothing to hold them together. Housing departments; children's officers, doctors, nurses, psychologists, the police, the probation service, the welfare officers, and of course the schools may all be involved in some of the cases. The child and its family are the subject of study and concern from innumerable professional and voluntary agencies.

The schools and the education officer have a central part to play. Basically the problem is to get at the factors impeding educational and social progress : they may of course stem from the school itself, from the home or from the child. If the education officer can weld together the forces called here special services he will have made a major contribution. Fundamentally his objective will be to reduce administrative complication arising from compartmentalism and to encourage co-operation in the field without the need for reference back up the ladders of power. Men and women associating together regularly in team-working in a district can quickly come to terms with the problem. This is not the same thing as solving it, but it is a start. Internal coherence of this kind can not only make headway within the education service but make it easier to link up with other similarly orientated services.

A co-operating team of school doctor, nurse, psychologist, social worker and education welfare officer can, in association with the schools, evolve together a system of analysing causes, detecting patterns, providing aid without bureaucracy, preventing recurrence and giving advice on legal and corrective treatment if necessary. They can join regularly with colleagues in housing and children's department, with police and probation service to pursue the wider implications of their work. These implications take us well beyond what is now known as special services, but it is there that the ripple must begin and spread outwards.

Further education

We have so far been concerned with the compulsory sector of education, the side that has largely grown up out of the desire of the state to have educated and responsible citizens. Further education has its roots in voluntary action—the desire of men to qualify themselves either vocationally or culturally for the world they live in and the wish of industry to recruit skilled men for their growing technical needs. Relatively recently the state has seen the connection between national prosperity and technical education and has begun to set the pace. For years the local education authorities pioneered and during recent years responded fully to all the national demands. Now, changed grant conditions coupled with intensified national pressures have begun to make the task look formidable. The painful readjustments arising from new solutions now being sought will play a growing part in the work of further education officers.

The term includes as well as technical education, the training of teachers, awards to students, adult education and evening institutes, youth and community work and the youth employment service. This is a vast and sprawling range of services loosely related by the age of those who enjoy them. To describe them in a short space is to invite disaster but the briefest sketch will give some idea of the size of the task and of the need for imaginative administration.

Whichever way you look at the colleges of further education they are various. Courses—full-time; sandwich; day-release; block release; evenings. Levels—post-graduate, advanced, intermediate and school level. Examinations—degrees, diplomas and certificates awarded by the CNAA, the City and Guilds, the Professional Bodies and the DES, the Royal Society of Arts, the Regional Examining Boards, the University Matriculation Boards and the colleges themselves. As to subjects, advanced full-time courses are a tiny fraction of the whole but in one region with 80 colleges there are these: in engineering 33 courses, 22 different types (civil, mechanical, production, electrical, chemical and so on); in architecture, planning and building 16 courses (11 types); metallurgy, chemistry and biology 15 (7 types); mining 1; mathematics and statistics 1; physics 3; pharmacy 3; textiles and clothing 7; nautical and marine studies 6; printing and photography 5; public health and welfare 10; food and institutional management 23 (13 types);

business studies, commerce, languages and administration 41 (23 types); art and design 18 (14 types).

A range of subjects from hairdressing to electronics produces problems whether the aim is designing a new college or new equipment, servicing and staffing establishments, or finding the money to finance it all. These are the crucial points of technical education together with regional co-operation with other authorities and with industry. Responsiveness to industry's needs is the tradition: the needs change rapidly and so must the training. The result, then, is constant pressure to start new courses, constant need to scrutinize the content and value of existing ones. Textiles and mining dominated the region described above not many years ago: now they form a meagre part of the whole.

So in all this there is a recipe for potential chaos. Add to it the historical development: technical institutes being set up and growing out of local pride and in recent years principals' salaries being geared to the numbers and grades of students enrolled and the result is a tendency towards competition rather than co-operation. The need both nationally and locally is to rationalize; to control new growth and cut back where necessary, but to do so without destroying the enthusiasm and initiative of those seeking to develop and expand.

At advanced level regional co-ordination is organized. The Regional Staff Inspector, advised by the Regional Advisory Council, makes decisions about new courses in line with national regulations and the Council may undertake periodic surveys of the pattern of provision for particular industries. For other courses co-operation tends to be casual and somewhat sketchy. But the further education officer is much concerned with regional matters—serving on committees and meeting with neighbouring authorities and with HMI.

Apart from approval of courses there is regional consultation on salaries of part-time teachers and the precise grading of the multiplicity of classes, fees to students, and inter-authority payments for students attending colleges outside their own area. Increasingly these matters are being settled nationally but local circumstances need to be taken into account and there is always likely to be some regional discretion. The Regional Advisory Council is a convenient forum for authorities and representatives of teachers' associations, universities, industry and HMI to meet to discuss these affairs, but in some regions other bodies, more narrowly based, deal with salaries and inter-authority payments: those who pay the piper like to call the tune and it may be a matter of *ad hoc* meetings of local education authority representatives. On fees there may be little formal consultation at all, though it is clearly highly desirable that there should not be big discrepancies between the charges in different areas, particularly as the fees charged by one authority may be paid, in the form of student grants, by another.

There are plenty of problems within the authority itself. Expansion costs money and there may be regular confrontations between officer and principal on numbers of staff required and amounts and costs of new equipment. The annual revenue estimates are a reality in further education where each college has its own individual needs, and the governors are a much more powerful force in the negotiations leading to their approval by the education committee.

The governors and their advisory committees will have strong representation from industry and commerce, and the stronger the links with industry the better the further education is likely to be. Increasingly many of the links are formal and organized—the Industrial Training Boards, for instance, have added a new dimension—but much contact is likely to be casual and informal. The principal and his staff are the main link but frequently the further education officer comes into the picture : the first request for a new course may come to the officer who will have to decide at which college it can be put on; new ventures, such as day-release for new types of student, may call for an official approach to industry.

A proposal for a new course cannot be considered in isolation. What facilities exist already, in the authority and outside it? The question is better answered if the use made of college premises is regularly measured by room-loading exercises and if all courses are reviewed annually to weed out those that are ailing. Can the course be fitted in to what exists already? Will the facilities measure up to the requirements of the appropriate examining body? If not, how far can the college be prepared in advance for a course that may not run, through lack of numbers? When the Diploma in Art and Design was introduced authorities were faced with a dilemma of a kind that has since grown more frequent.

Only a limited number of colleges were to be allowed to offer these courses and a visiting committee toured all the applicant colleges to advise on what was needed before approval could be considered. It was a matter of judgement whether to take the risk of providing staff, accommodation and equipment for courses that might never run. Similarly the Council for National Academic Awards make preliminary visits and indicate what is needed before applicants have any chance of success. These are financial questions of some complexity, in view of the pooling arrangements for advanced courses.

But the major issues in advanced further education are those stemming from the Robbins Report. In 1963 the Robbins Committee recommended an extension of the means by which a number of large technical colleges had been given university status : most colleges would continue under local control but others would federate as autonomous polytechnics. The government accepted the idea of polytechnics but did not agree to extend the university principle any further : the polytechnics would be given new methods of government and more independence but would remain under local auspices. The basis of the arrangement—agreeing an annual sum of expenditure for the college and allowing freedom as to how it should be spent—gives more freedom to the polytechnics than many education committees themselves enjoy, so it is not entirely clear how the venture will fare, though its chances of success are improved by the fact that almost all expenditure on these colleges will be shared amongst all authorities through the pool.

The Robbins Report also recommended that the colleges of education should, with existing university departments of education, become part of the university structure. And again this was not accepted, though the Weaver Report proposed administrative arrangements that put the colleges on the very brink of local control. In teacher training the shift of administrative work and power is in some ways less than in technical education because the local authorities had less real control to lose. Ever since 1944 the Government has—for obvious strategic reasons—kept tight control over the expansion, staffing, training pattern and general standards of the training colleges. Governing bodies have been given very considerable freedom and local financial control over estimates has been light because of the inflationary effect of the pooling system which makes it appear that nobody pays. Staffing ratios and salary levels have long been settled nationally.

In fact the aim in most local education offices has been to provide architectural, legal and financial services, to foster links with the schools and to give advice and support in dealing with the problems of running residential establishments for high-spirited young adults. This general relationship will remain. So will two other links : teaching practice for students in the schools and involvement of the colleges in the in-service training of the authority's teachers.

Awards to students for designated courses of degree equivalent at universities and colleges of further education are largely governed by national regulation. So are those for college of education students. But there are many courses below this top-level for which authorities have to make up their own rules and many complicated problems arising from the discretionary elements even in the national regulations. The peculiar balance of decision between costs, possible precedents, individual need and national interest is not easy. No one has yet satisfactorily resolved such questions as whether to give grants for denominational theological training or whether the level of grant should depend on the standard of the course or on the age of the student. Students of the same age as university students following courses just as expensive though not as academically high-powered really need grants of the same size. Yet these same courses may have students of seventeen or sixteen : should they not have the same grant? If so what of those who stay on at school to that age? The cost would be prohibitive. If an arbitrary limit of eighteen is fixed students of different ages following the same course may get different rates of grant. It bristles with possible anomalies. The great pressure for quick decisions and quick payment of grants at certain times of the year, the false starts, failures and erratic behaviour of certain students, the difficulty of assessing the standards of hundreds of different institutions offering courses for which people apply for grants—from drama schools to colleges of occupational therapy—all these make this far from the easiest sector in the education department.

The rest of further education is the home of the poor relations. Adult education, youth and community work and the youth employment service can lay just about equal claim to the name of Cinderella. Not everyone means the same thing by adult education. At one time it clearly meant liberal adult education of the kind provided by the WEA and the University Extra-Mural Departments, the Responsible Bodies. The night schools were places where people could try to get qualifications to improve their job prospects : even when they were dignified by the title of evening institutes the image remained. Now when secondary education for all, the growth of technical colleges with full-time and part-time day courses, and increased leisure for many more people have transformed the situation, the evening institutes exist primarily to provide a wide range of recreational classes from dressmaking to languages and motor-car maintenance. So a modern definition of adult education has to include the evening institutes.

They are by far the biggest providers. By 1967 over one million four hundred thousand adult education students attended local authority evening institutes, compared with under a quarter of a million elsewhere. As they are usually held in schools they are a most economical proposition even though the fees charged represent only a tiny proportion of the cost of even the teachers' salaries. Attempts to find separate accommodation—so that, for example, more day-time classes can be held—have not been outstandingly successful, though some enterprising authorities have been able to convert old schools very satisfactorily. So shared use of premises is one of the further education officer's problems. To make a member of the day school staff the evening institute principal may be to exchange one problem for another: it may ease possible tensions but it may fail to secure someone who can make the necessary change of atmosphere from school to adult world.

The atmosphere and tone of the evening institutes will depend heavily on the enthusiasm and initiative of the further education officer. It is a world in which tradition dies hard and if he preserves the conventional style no one on the committee or even in the public is likely to worry very much. But at least part of their growing popularity is the result of a changed style—informal arrangements over enrolment, no registers, cups of tea, members' committees, theatre visits and other activities beyond the actual classes, perhaps a single fee covering club membership of a centre offering as well as classes a common room, a library and a coffee bar. In conditions of intensive competition for premises few authorities are likely to be able to build new adult education centres—perhaps the most to be hoped for is the modest addition to secondary schools allowed by the regulations or exceptionally an adult wing designed for use by day and evening students.

But a more decisive factor still is the recruitment and training of teachers. There are fewer than 500 full-time adult education teachers in the whole country: the scope is obviously limited when so much is evening work. Very few authorities feel able to insist on even a brief preliminary training course as a condition of appointment for the part-timers who predominate: indeed because of the numbers and the concentrated evening time-span of their operation there is rarely any on-the-job training or inspection. Those who wish to introduce training have to contend with dangers of making recruitment even more difficult and they will find it hard to convince many people that a qualification for teaching school-children is not enough for adult work.

The historical origins of adult education have left a curious legacy: in the local authorities a kind of puritanism that looks with suspicion at the non-vocational, and in the Responsible Bodies a strict avoidance of the vocational in favour of the academic and the cultural. The DES, in periods of financial difficulty, and some local committees, may wish to discriminate in the fees to be charged against purely recreational classes though this often breaks down in the extreme difficulty of defining the classes to be singled out in this way. Most further education officers seek the smallest possible distinction in the fees charged between the various subjects. They also seek to co-ordinate the LEA's programme with that of the local Responsible Bodies. In most areas the LEA augments the subsidy provided by the DES to these extra-mural classes but a jointly planned programme is rare. The independent traditions extend to higher teachers' salary scales and more heavily subsidized students' fees outside the LEA world which perhaps more than anything else hinders full co-ordination.

There has been a more encouraging advance in residential adult education. As well as eight colleges offering full-time courses there are over thirty—mainly LEA-controlled—which offer short courses, and the greatest growth has been not so much in traditional cultural subjects as in management and industrial relations conferences and seminars. The mass media have a potential as yet only partly realized in adult education : the new Open University is an imaginative attempt to use television to overcome cost problems by this cheap and convenient means of communication and local radio offers less dramatic but useful opportunities for experiment.

But so far adult education has remained peripheral. The National Institute of Adult Education, for many years a patient, sympathetic and tactful friend to all the partners in the enterprise, express the situation well in a recent year-book 'The top professionals and the workers are missing'. A cynic might conclude that because the most influential members of the community find no need for adult education, and the great majority of the voters are not involved, successive governments have never supported it with conviction.

There has been no lack of recent political concern about the youth service. The growing impact of the young on society has made 'youth' a strongly emotive label, part scare, part watchword. Further education officers, hampered by a conventional upbringing and operating in a somewhat inflexible administrative set-up, have not found themselves notably better equipped to meet the challenge than the churches, social services, well-meaning amateurs or the government. Attitudes to youth change almost as fast as the pace of life so it is possible now to patronize the Albemarle Report as old-fashioned a very few years after its publication. Yet scarcely anyone before Albemarle got beyond deploring the amount of money young people had to spend or helping to keep them off the streets by providing table-tennis in a hut.

Administrators need intermediate objectives, and the duties bestowed by the 1944 Act were vague to say the least. 'Dedication', 'leadership' and 'service' may have been the ultimate aims of the youth service but the practice tended to centre on short-term objectives so practical as to be almost sterile. Albemarle's 'association', 'training' and 'challenge' were recognizable targets which could be turned into specific projects without too much strain on the imagination. The impact on local committees resulting in greater financial provision and on the Government resulting in a national building programme seeking to bring local education authorities and voluntary organizations together to plan their provision seems small only when measured against the need. Albemarle and the subsequent Bessey Report on training part-time leaders helped to strengthen local authorities' contribution and to give them worthwhile if not earth-shaking aims. The relative failure of the voluntary organizations to advance has been no more than confirmation of the obsolescence of the conventional notion of the voluntary principle.

This is perhaps the central problem in the youth service for the further education officer. Many voluntary organizations have, of course, out-stripped their statutory partners in enterprise and vision. But the voluntary principle has shown itself too often in the provision of premises (either through philanthropy or devoted money-raising) by well-meaning bodies with terms of reference too narrow for a modern 'open' society: too often they have found themselves lacking financial resources—and sometimes the heart—to sustain ventures patently lacking attractive powers for those they sought to bring in. In the short-term the LEA may need to step into the breach financially, but a statutory version of the traditional, and unsuccessful, voluntary pattern can hardly offer a permanent solution. In the long-term voluntary help will have to play its part in other ways than offering individual ventures, whether in need of subsidy or not.

For example, local communities as a whole—including as partners, not sponsors, the voluntary bodies—might increasingly be concerned in the management of institutions and organizations financed by the local authority. Second, the 'challenge' aspect of Albemarle could turn more and more in the direction of community service by young people. And third, the artificial barriers between youth and adult community activities could gradually disappear. A more valid criticism of the Albemarle ethos than its alleged leanings towards club work as opposed to the natural leanings of young people might be in its effect—if not its intention—of isolating an age-group. It should surprise no one that if the basis of association is no more than similarity of age the range of activities of youth club members should be reduced to fairly low common denominators—or that many of them should prefer to do them in glossier, commercial surroundings.

The Report of the Youth Service Development Council in 1969 emphasized this kind of orientation in proposing a new title, Youth and Community Service. It looks for closer links with the social services and with trade unions and industry, and a change from the club approach, especially for the over-16s, with an emphasis on counselling services.

Some LEAs have already reshaped their services in this way. They may also have seen and practised the distinction made by the Report between community provision—buildings—community organization—co-ordinating existing voluntary effort—and community development—helping groups to identify their needs and work towards achieving them. But elsewhere a few community centres, sometimes an uneasy amalgam of adult education, youth work and social events, may be the extent of their commitment.

Many educationists and committee members are frankly unsure how much this new thinking has to do with education. The line is shadowy but there can be little doubt that the newer approaches are in fact essentially educational: perhaps more so than the old. However, the education service has given this work low priority in terms of money. Its successes have been spectacular (such as the Cambridgeshire village colleges) when securely based on traditional educational foundations, but unconvincing when slanted towards the acute social needs of an urban community.

Another service on the social frontiers of education reflects only slightly less uncertainty. Some authorities have never assumed responsibility for the youth employment service, and some who have have under-estimated its relevance to the main stream of education. Yet its officers are amongst the most zealous advocates of education, providing a great deal else besides good careers advice to school-leavers. They are an essential link between schools, further education and the outside world and when the school leaving age is raised their value will become even clearer.

Sites and buildings

The three main sectors we have considered have been operational policy-making branches. Sites and buildings work is different: it is important, and costly, and highly influential but it is essentially a service to the other branches. It can in some ways be the hardest for the education officer recruited from teaching because so different from what he has experienced before.

The range of skills, and the amount of knowledge required are substantial; the frustrations and complexities are equally formidable; and the financial responsibility is as great as anywhere in the service. Describing it is a problem, particularly in a brief space. So, since the bulky Building Code of the Department of Education and Science gives a thorough exposition of procedures and factual data, this note will refer only to a few of the main elements in the job of the senior officer responsible.

First, planning. After the logistical exercise has been carried out in conjunction with the housing authorities a school of appropriate size and type will be included in the local development plan in one of its many revisions. The proposals and needs of the denominational authorities must be borne in mind to avoid overlap. From there it must take a more difficult step into a national building programme. A site has to be ear-marked of regulation size and suited to its purpose. Once it is in a programme a public notice as prescribed in Section 13 of the 1944 Act has to be displayed for two months and any objections considered by the Secretary of State.

Most of the processes are stereotyped and inevitable but they can combine to produce disaster if they are not synchronized. After the expiry of the notices the stages are planning approval; educational planning leading to a brief and schedule of accommodation from which the architect can produce sketch plans; revision and final plans; architect's work preparatory to going to tender; tendering, acceptance and signing the contract; and construction work. But stage by stage completion of each before starting the next is not normally possible. The exercise is ready made for network analysis to show which stages will take how long and require what resources: critical path analysis for instance can show the quickest and most economical disposition of time and forces. When many jobs are in hand simultaneously the exercise is even more essential. Educational planning may well be the longest, most crucial factor, for instance, so a start can be made before building programme approval; the quest for planning approval can be begun before the expiry of the public notices and so on. For most elements the likely time can be forecast in advance and if for some reason the time-table is inadequate then it is possible after analysis to make a convincing case to the committee for short-circuiting the normal procedure. For example the normal, democratic process of open tendering may have to be set aside in favour of negotiating tenders with particular firms or firms from a list approved by the council. Not only time but money is a crucial factor: an increasing hazard with open tendering is that none of the tenders may come within the cost limits set by the Department and the architect's estimate.

Apart from planning, the education officer's chief concern is the preparatory work leading to the architect's sketch plans. The design may be very complicated and the cost enormous for large secondary schools and colleges of further education. The administrator has to ensure three things: that the building is planned as a whole with a clearly defined objective in mind; that the project comes as far as possible within time and cost limits; and that educational considerations always come first in the design. In all three he is a vital link between the various partners in the enterprise. The lay-out of the building; the juxtaposition of rooms; the range and characteristics of specialist teaching rooms and the communal and administrative facilities have to be discussed with specialist advisers, HMI, medical officers, the teachers who will use the building and of course the architect. Reconciling all these points of view is not always easy particularly within harsh cost limits.

School building has to embody educational characteristics that will stand the test of twenty years of time. It must be advanced enough to help the work of progressive teachers but not so revolutionary as to provoke hostility from the less radical professionals or from education committees. No one can safely generalize on so contentious a matter but there are a few principles that seem to be widely accepted:

1   a flexible teaching environment—that is
    a   setting teaching free from formality by giving large spaces in which a variety of different activities can take place, and
    b   allowing in design and construction for future changes in organization or approach;
2   a lessening of the institutional in favour of the personal;
3   attention to the aesthetic—good design and proportion, colour and shape can have a good influence in themselves.

The philosophy of the institution and the age and qualities of the users should permeate everyone's thinking about the design. Each new school or college is an individual venture but that does not preclude sound general principles being laid down in advance. Indeed everybody gains from clear and detailed exposition of the principles to be followed. Thereafter each new job adds something or modifies the statement. At a prosaic level the statement is invaluable as a reminder and a check-list; it provides continuity when staff changes occur; and above all it ensures that mistakes are not repeated. If an assessment is made periodically after each job there may be less of the frequently heard tirades—after the event—about the folly of architects.

The consortium is the modern answer to the struggle against costs and time. In its fullest development groups of authorities co-operate to fix standard prefabricated components and to correlate building programmes. The DES Development Group has also had some success in demonstrating new approaches within the framework of normal building regulations and procedures. The achievements of the Department as a whole in setting standards and stimulating new ideas are of great value to local administrators. Many of them think there would be still greater benefit from relaxation of the regulations. Prescribed minimum standards are understandable : so are cost limits. But is there any reason why within these limits authorities should not be free to lay out their money to best advantage according to their allocation in the building programmes? The freedom extended to minor works building would seem by now capable of extension to the whole range.

Furniture and equipment are not ancillaries. They have always been too important in the minds of good architects and good educators to leave until after the building was planned. Nowadays one can claim without straining too far after paradox that the furniture should come first. The combined effects of standardized construction and the need for flexibility tend to produce schools of austere design with ceilings of uniform height and containing all the services so that partition walls can be knocked about as required. This standard plan can produce a functional neutrality— something nearly suitable for everything and tailor-made for nothing—and a most uninspiring teaching environment. So furniture and equipment can make all the difference. The designer begins with the educational activities that will be going on, then the equipment they need and the amount of space required to go round them. He has more freedom to design the furniture than to plan the rest of the building. And the education officer's role as link-man, the man who confronts the architect with educational need, is more important than ever.

So the sites and buildings officer has to be up-to-date with all the developments in educational technology, the machinery that is on the way to transforming approaches to learning and teaching. Technology has shown new ways of making things memorable and also of making best use of scarce resources of skilled manpower. The administrator's function here is not merely choosing with his teacher colleagues the best kinds of equipment in terms of value for money, though this is important. He will probably play a decisive part in deciding whether a particular type of machine moves from the category of 'interesting idea' to 'available if requested' or 'standard equipment'. Then he will try to find the best (most versatile, longest-lasting, easiest-to-use, cheapest) example of the type and, just as important, try to get the money to buy it. He will be concerned to see that equipment issued is properly used, with preliminary training if need be, that its supply is planned, and that its performance is evaluated.

Tape-recorders, radio, film, television (network and closed circuit), language laboratories, teaching machines. These have already brought about a change of name from audio-visual aids to educational technology. Outsiders may wistfully imagine the replacement of teachers by machines: teachers may emphasize that these are not substitutes for, but adjuncts to, the pedagogic art. The future of educational technology probably lies somewhere between these two extremes, but there can be no doubt of its central part in the planning of new schools and colleges and in the remodelling of old ones.

5

Office organization

This will be a short chapter. One reason is that good education officers, though conscious of the importance of efficient organization, are not obsessed by it. In social services only a sterile and debased administration is pre-occupied with its own machinery. Another reason is that many education officers have little influence over their office organization. The new entrant, of course, can expect to have little, but even chief education officers tend not to be their own masters in this.

Staff gradings and numbers are usually fixed by establishment committees or their equivalent outside the education service, and they tend to have regard to standard patterns throughout local government rather than individual departmental needs. Traditions and the expectations of the staff association also play their part in restricting discretion. The education committee are naturally concerned: sub-committee chairmen for instance want their own branches to be effective (and usually as large as possible). The physical shape of the building is also important: antiquated former solicitor's offices are not the best places to undertake redeployment of staff.

So we find a strong tradition of putting up with what exists. Unfortunately not only the officers but the schools and colleges and the public may have to put up with the results, too. At least the education officer can recognize the organizational needs of his service and try to be in a position to reshape it if the opportunity arises.

The basis of sub-division

Because of the predominance of committee influence on education it may well be that the office organization matches the pattern of the sub-committees of the education committee. Thus if there are sub-committees for primary education, secondary education, further education, special services and sites and buildings there may well be a basic sub-division of the office under assistant education officers into these elements. If the education committee has a policy and finance sub-committee this may match the place in the scheme of things of the chief education officer and his deputy. There is much in favour of this: education officers serve education committees and the committees make the policy. However it is not necessarily the best basis for organization.

Much administrative work is not directly linked with the committee's activities; committees operate only intermittently and a good deal has to be done between meetings. Sub-committee structures are likely to reflect the committee's traditional concern with institutional management, supervising and supporting schools and colleges, rather than policy-making. For obvious reasons it may be that the sub-committee pattern is not ideal, and as the education officer is unlikely to be able to shape the committee structure exactly according to his wishes, he may be unwise to match the office organization too closely to it.

Quite apart from sub-committee patterns many education officers tend to sub-divide their staffs according to the types of institutions that have to be managed. Institutional management is an important part of educational administration and it may well be that a basic sub-division similar to that assumed in the last chapter—primary and secondary schools, special schools and related services, further education—will be found convenient. Even on the assumption that institutional management is the main purpose of the organization, however, there are complications.

Many education office activities lend themselves better to a functional pattern of organization rather than one based on blocks of institutions. The work of the sites and buildings branch described in the previous chapter is an obvious example. And important parts of the office's work were omitted for the sake of simplicity: salaries, accounts, supplies, transport, provision of meals and milk. These and the appointment of teachers and other staff are common to all the schools and colleges. It would theoretically be possible to sub-divide a whole office on the basis of functions rather than institutions with AEOs for Personnel, Sites and Buildings, Institutional Management, Finance and so on. Yet there are such fundamental differences between the requirements of schools and further education that at least this division by institutions is needed in most offices at senior, policy-making or policy-influencing, level.

The problem becomes more manageable if it is thought of in terms of operational and service sections. Schools, further education are operational: sites and buildings, staffing, accounts are service activities. There is not necessarily any distinction in status between the officers concerned. For example Sites and Buildings may well be so big and important as to merit at least equal ranking with Schools and Further Education as a sub-division under an AEO. Yet it remains different in kind from the others. Service functions other than sites and buildings may call for sub-divisions of lesser standing than these major units, but not necessarily; much would depend on circumstances. The appointment and distribution of teaching staff, if extended to all institutions including further education would be an enormously important responsibility meriting a very senior appointment.

The dangers of sub-division according to service functions mainly arise from half-hearted implementation. If it is to be done then it must be done thoroughly. For example if a personnel section is set up, for teachers and other staff, there is little purpose in doing it if the resulting section is sub-divided according to primary, secondary and further education, particularly if each is effectively responsible to a senior officer in one of these main units. Indeed there are positive disadvantages apart from divided responsibility: for instance a member of a further education unit responsible for its own staffing matters may tackle other jobs than, say, the appointment of non-teaching staff. If he is removed to form part of a staffing section, he leaves behind those extra duties for someone else to do, while he himself may be under-employed if he is confined only to further education non-teaching staff in his new post.

This brings us to the phenomenon known as 'Fred's patch'. In the staffing section, Fred knows all about caretakers, Joe deals with laboratory technicians, Florence with welfare assistants and so on. Clearly this is psychologically satisfying in that one person can see through from start to finish all the business concerned with his own little sector: he knows he is dealing with people not just processes. But supposing Fred is away—who then deals with caretakers? And what about the salary structure: if Joe gets more money for doing an identical job for technicians to the one Florence does for welfare assistants, there is something wrong. It is surely important that the difficult parts of the exercise should be done by those who carry greatest theoretical responsibility.

The full rigour of the logical alternative—organization of work by division of the tasks for all staff into stages of the operation— may not be desirable. It is hard to retain interest if you are restricted to one assembly-line function. So some flexibility has to be retained : this can be achieved fairly easily in a large office by organizing the work on group lines, with inter-change of functions within the group according to the circumstances. In smaller offices it may be less desirable to set up service units.

But educational administration is by no means entirely institutional management. The institutions carry out parts of the authority's policy. The policy itself when articulated in plans can be expressed in terms of objectives and ideally the organization should be shaped with these in mind. The system of programme-planning-budgeting can be used to focus on these objectives : for instance, through listing current activities, grouping them in logical clusters, considering the needs they are intended to meet, measuring their costs and effectiveness and then considering whether different activities might not meet the objective better.

This method can not only help with review of policy but also show which groupings of resources, including office staff, should combine for greater effectiveness. It can raise sights above the level of simply providing and running institutions towards the reasons why they are provided. But it is a device for raising relevant questions rather than providing answers.

Objectives in education cannot often be pinned down; they may overlap or conflict with each other. The desire to achieve a good office organization may thus lead to compromise solutions to avoid conflict, whereas in fact the conflict may be necessary to avoid stagnation. This suggests that an education office cannot safely rely on traditional ladder or family-tree models. Something more dynamic is needed.

Flow of work

Hierarchical family-tree organization is to be found in education offices as much as anywhere else, though the application is probably less formal and rigid than in other local government departments. In this the education office is probably enjoying the worst of both worlds, for of course the orthodox hierarchical structure depends for its effectiveness on thorough and systematic execution.

Education seems better suited to organization based on looser groupings with capacity for growth and relatively free inter-action. Senior administrators, recruited from common rooms, are more attuned to notions of *primus inter pares* than precise degrees of seniority, and they have regular contact with schools and colleges who conduct their affairs in this way. Then too, the work has such a wide variety of somewhat dissimilar branches that a sub-division into many smaller independent groups rather than a few larger ones with smaller dependencies seems logical. And the work changes rapidly in the various branches, so that a loose framework in which a particular element can grow or be reduced is desirable.

For the top management the CEO may conduct affairs entirely on the basis of a one-to-one relationship with each of his senior colleagues, keeping the affairs of each separate from the others. This places a heavy responsibility on him, as a co-ordinator, apart from being unhelpful to the notion of co-operative working. He may on the other hand wish to settle all major matters collectively, as in Cabinet meetings. The danger here is of blurred lines of responsibility and possible resentment at the general discussion of what may be felt to be personal responsibilities. Yet, if care is taken in the selection of subjects for this treatment and in the handling of them, it is an effective and natural way of conducting affairs. Regular (but not too frequent) meetings of this kind can also encourage useful meetings of AEOs, or Deputy and AEOs, to see that separate sections do not pursue wildly different or isolationist policies.

For most of the time, however, the flow of work at this level has to be conducted directly between CEO—Deputy; CEO—AEO; and sometimes Deputy—AEO. If the pure doctrine of the family-tree organization ends there it becomes much easier to answer the vital question of whether everything is expected to originate from the top and pass down the line, or whether the initiative is at the junior end. For of course there need be much less anxiety about the implications of maximum delegation if the number of transactions at different levels is reduced. There can be two-way working at the top level, and then two-way working directly between AEOs and the leaders of whatever sub-groups are established.

Office organization

This kind of organization is not:

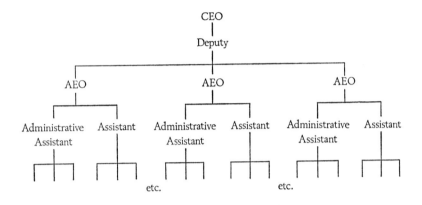

but rather something like this:

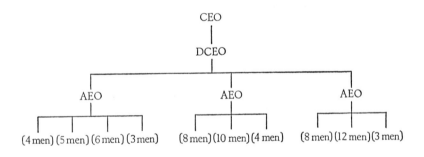

The family-tree can only work satisfactorily if the process of sub-division of responsibility is carried out fully and consistently. Suppose for instance an AEO in charge of primary and secondary schools has two administrative assistants, one for primary and one for secondary education: the logical need is for separate supporting sections for primary and secondary schools. Yet it may make better sense to have a combined schools section so as to make best use of resources, and to have one man in charge of it.

The logical way would be:

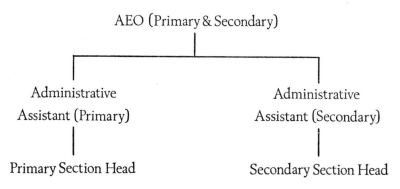

AEO (Primary & Secondary)

Administrative Assistant (Primary)

Administrative Assistant (Secondary)

Primary Section Head

Secondary Section Head

There may be difficulties in:

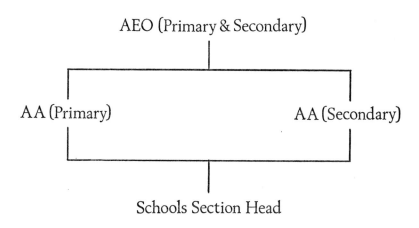

AEO (Primary & Secondary)

AA (Primary)

AA (Secondary)

Schools Section Head

If there is a full flow of work through the two administrative assistants the Section Head has the burden of correlating them and of apportioning time to the demands of each. Since many matters will be common to both primary and secondary it is not entirely practical to transmit everything through the administrative assistants and the natural route will be between the two men who have responsibilities to both sectors—the AEO and the Schools Section Head. This can lead to feelings of irritation at being by-passed and of course under-use of talents. Yet it would seem wrong to split the section into two and lose the advantage of pooling resources in a section in which the two halves have much work in common: for example, both may deal with governors' and managers' meetings and the transfer of pupils from primary to secondary school.

Careful examination may suggest that the benefits of the hierarchical system are more illusory than real. They are based on the theory that at each level the officer concerned personally plays a part, initiating, deciding upon or amending. In fact many of the stages of the operation are quite automatic, the mere time-wasting process of passing through another pair of hands. The initiator of an item for a committee agenda may be a very junior officer indeed, yet, particularly if those senior to him hold their rank through responsibility for another section of the work, as is usual, no one may know more about the matter than he. So the item travels on, acquiring more and more sets of initials, until it reaches someone senior enough to be concerned with it as an aspect of general policy or as a piece of prose. There is much to be said for legitimizing the natural processes and creating short, direct lines of communication and flow of work.

Yet it is unrealistic to think of local government offices with no hierarchy. Perhaps basic responsibilities can be redistributed to take some account of the degree of seniority. Too often in education offices (as in some schools) certain responsibilities traditionally attach to certain posts, but of course times change and regular review is needed. Other jobs have grown up over the years into a hotch-potch. Only a full-scale job analysis can throw up anomalies such as this. Change is rarely popular, but even if a gradual policy of adjustment is followed as people leave it is as well to be prepared before vacancies actually occur.

Even so there will be many occasions when any kind of fixed formal pattern of working is out-of-place. Co-operation between groups of officers, sometimes in different branches, will often be necessary, and these groups will need to form and re-form according to the particular problem to be solved. We shall consider the team and some of its wider functions in administration in later chapters. Within the education office the project team can allow the ladder hierarchy to be retained for the purposes appropriate to it, but permit direct consultation between officers who need to work together for particular jobs.

Something like this happens in most offices but usually in an informal and rather haphazard fashion. Small units may be able to manage this way but bigger ones cannot. The wish to humanize large organizations often leads to an attempted person-to-person approach to matters of this kind, but the result is usually mere confusion. The best basis for good personal relations in a big organization is a well-organized system of working : this makes time for the personal and keeps tempers sweeter.

A deliberate well-ordered policy of project-team working also recognizes the shifting nature of relationships. People who wish to know where they stand in a big organization may be the victims of muddle, but they may also be seeking the unattainable if what they are looking for is a once-for-all definition of their status. Hierarchical standing is one thing but the shifting pattern of working relationships is something quite different.

Professional and advisory staff

An important question, particularly in bigger offices, is that of the function and relative status of educational advisory staff. (They may be called inspectors, advisers or organizers : the names vary partly according to tradition and partly according to the relationship envisaged between these officers and the teachers. Adviser is the term used here.) They are usually recruited from experienced teachers and have good academic qualifications but of course no administrative background. Their duties will include advising and inspecting individual teachers, advising heads of schools, organizing courses and conferences, advising on the planning of new building according to their specialist knowledge, and perhaps interviewing and appointing probationer teachers and advising governors and managers on more senior appointments.

There may be only one or two advisers in which case they will work quite informally with the AEOs and may advise the CEO direct. In bigger offices their role and status *vis-à-vis* AEOs or administrative assistants may need clarification. Salary questions affect the issue. Advisers' salary scales are negotiated by the Soulbury Committee, which tends to relate its recommendations to those made for the teaching profession. Administrators' salaries are negotiated within the general local government structure which is in no way related to awards to the teaching profession. Thus the salary relationship tends to change fairly frequently and can cause endless trouble.

Status apart, the place of the advisers in the organization has to be worked out. They may be involved in administrative jobs (appointing staff, planning buildings); they need clerical help; they need to fit their activities within the general policy; and they need to be kept informed about developments outside their own particular sphere. If there is a Chief Adviser there may be a separate operational unit which simplifies problems of administrative relationship and provides an obvious link for the purpose of integrating advisers' work with policy as a whole. If there is no Chief Adviser they may work to an AEO or the Deputy. Whatever the arrangements special care is needed in securing integration. For one thing they are most large offices' main link with the schools and colleges. Even more important, however, is that they should be used not simply to advise teachers or plan specialist accommodation. They can be most valuable of all in advising the education officer about the basic purposes of the service and the techniques by which they can be achieved.

Advisers and administrative colleagues tend to unite on one point : in requiring as much delegation of authority as possible in order to exercise their responsibilities in a way their professional status requires. The tension between professionalism and organization is never easy, but the nature of the government of local education presents this dilemma in an acute form. Individual committee members, whatever the size of the authority, tend to raise specific questions with the CEO before, at or after committee meetings. There is a built-in tendency for him (and perhaps them) to feel that he ought to know the answers, all of them, himself. Yet there quickly comes a time when it is a sheer physical impossibility for him to attend to matters of detail. In some offices the conflict may be permanently unresolved, an uneasy tension with the CEO trying to keep one jump ahead and anticipate every enquiry, to know more about everything than anyone else. In others the organization and method of working allow for a situation in which subordinate professional officers are accepted as advisers to the sub-committees within their own sphere of operation. The CEO may not always attend the sub-committee meetings himself : if he does he may not act as adviser on all matters arising—he may not 'take the meeting' as the administrators say—but may rather sit in at the meeting informing himself about the work of the sub-committee and on members' views and intervening if some general issue of policy should arise.

Basically this is a question of attitude. Does delegation involve the men on the spot taking responsibility and initiative, accepting the onus of keeping the CEO informed on matters likely to be raised at a higher level or to affect general policy? Or does it mean that the CEO himself initiates everything and fixes in advance and in each instance the limits within which his assistants are to act on his behalf? With the second of these approaches it may suit the CEO to have all his senior colleagues, including his deputy, working within specified sectors, with himself acting as a co-ordinator. With the first he may achieve co-ordination through his deputy, leaving himself free to tackle major issues of policy, to plan ahead, to work with the Chairman of his committee in seeing that the essential objectives are kept in mind, to strengthen links with other departments and other committees of the council. One very important responsibility—to encourage the heads and teachers in schools and colleges, and support his own headquarters staff—he cannot delegate. That is his personal duty.

6

Administrative processes

Previous chapters, setting the scene, have looked at the context and the content of the education officer's work. We now turn to some of the characteristics. Administration is a two-way process: the good administrator neither indulges in fanciful thinking without regard to practical consequences, nor merely reacts to external stimuli. Sometimes he may seem to be in the grip of events, but there are very few processes in which he does not have the opportunity to make a positive contribution as well.

The two representative processes discussed here are chosen with this in mind. The first is relatively small, the kind that the beginner in administration may have to deal with; the second a major planning exercise in which he might, with experience, be asked to assist. The essential principles remain the same.

An application for a grant

Education officers in their time have to deal, either directly or indirectly, with many thousands of applications for grants, for university or further education, for boarding school education, for free meals or necessitous clothing. The pattern is the same: committee or national regulations are framed, income scales are devised and the administrator has to implement the authority's policy. There is more in it than meets the eye.

1 The quality of administration shows itself even before the application form comes in. Well-designed forms are not merely easier to fill-in; they are easier to handle. It will help the office staff

if the various forms used in the department conform as far as possible to a standard pattern, the surname, address and other particulars always appearing in the same relationship. It may also help the public for certain families will need to apply for a variety of different purposes as their children grow up. The questions asked should be clearly and simply phrased without jargon or stately Victorian words.

2   Immediate response to the form is important. Applications are usually a source of anxiety to the applicant and they deserve an acknowledgement. Any questions that need to be asked, either in clarification of information given or as supporting evidence from referees or college authorities should be asked at once. The way these questions are asked is important, too : a stereotyped form of enquiry may be necessary but there is no need for it to be semi-literate. The answers should be read as soon as received and pursued again if necessary. Otherwise when the senior officer or committee responsible come to make the decision they may find that an urgent decision is needed but that they lack essential information.

3   The officer immediately responsible will have to decide whether the matter is one for committee or whether it can be dealt with administratively. Decisions about decisions need to be taken quickly and at the lowest level possible, reserving the decisions themselves for the senior staff. It is wasteful to compose a memorandum to a senior officer merely to ask him whether the issue is one for committee or not. The need is for a policy file readily available with a full record of doubtful cases.

4   If the application does not appear to fall within existing categories of eligibility then another sort of decision is needed. A bureaucratic reaction is to write back unreflectingly to say that no grant is possible : a good organization provides for all possibilities to be considered. The policy file is again essential provided it is carefully dated. If the committee declined an identical application the previous week the applicant can be told politely that he is wasting his time. If the last instance was some years ago then the circumstances need revaluation.

5   The application will then have to be processed. The form and content of supporting material to be presented to the senior officer or committee deciding should be standardized as far as possible, to save their time and to make it easy to refer to key points. A balance has to be struck between wasting their time in hunting through files for relevant information and spending more time on documentation

than the item merits. Another balance is in the selection of material in any summary of the case.

6 The crucial stage is the decision itself. Written regulations may cover much of the ground but there may be other factors where personal judgement is needed. If the decision is to be made by a committee the presenting officer will put forward the facts fairly but will usually want to give his own opinion on the merits. His advice may take the form of reminding the committee of earlier, similar decisions, or of warning them of the dangers of creating a precedent. He cannot assume that because it has never happened it never should.

7 After the decision implementation is just as important. The applicant should be told as soon as possible, and if there is likely to be any delay in payment he should be told and told why. Politeness will be needed whatever the outcome, but particularly if the answer is no. Again, if at all possible the reasons for a negative answer should be given.

Even the simplest administrative operation can be handled well or badly. Apart from the importance to the individual these encounters with the public are important to the impression created by the department. The response must be well-ordered and objective but at the same time sympathetic; the handling must be swift yet accurate; there is a duty to the ratepayer as well as to the individual. Performance in an operation such as this can be a barometer of the administrative climate in the organization as a whole.

Secondary reorganization

We now turn to a very different problem : much bigger in scope and in its potential impact; more obviously dependent on planning; calling for more initiative from the education officer. This particular operation has been chosen because of its dramatic eruption on the educational scene and because it shows clearly in the inter-play of the various forces and groups involved the complex and fundamentally pragmatic nature of the education service. It is considered here purely as an administrative exercise and no comment is intended on the educational, still less the political, aspects of the question.

It is entirely characteristic that this major change should originate not in intensive Government-sponsored research, nor as a result of a national plan prepared by the DES but in the initiative of local education authorities. Comprehensive schools are not mentioned in the 1944 Act and it seems likely that its authors did not envisage them. Secondary education for all children was to be provided in schools 'sufficient in number, character and equipment' to provide instruction and training suitable to their 'different ages, abilities and aptitudes of the different periods for which they may be expected to remain at school'. Certainly the White Paper which preceded the act assumed three main types of school, grammar, technical and modern, and the Departmental circulars which followed it assumed the same. Yet certain LEAs—Coventry, London, Middlesex, Oldham and the West Riding—swam against the tide and proposed comprehensive schools in their development plans.

In most places first priority went to providing secondary modern schools as improved versions of the former senior elementaries. The debate began. A Ministry pamphlet in 1947 rehearsed the arguments though it assumed that the great majority of schools would be separate. The stern realities of roofs over heads preoccupied central and local authorities. A new government in 1951 decided that proposals to make comprehensive schools by closing grammar schools could not be approved : rural areas and new housing estates were assumed to be the natural growth points of all-purpose schools. Such other changes as there were occurred when no substantial building changes were needed so that the Minister had no power to intervene. Thus in 1957 Leicestershire changed the function of existing grammar and modern schools without Ministerial intervention.

So the organization of secondary education was very largely a question first of the interpretation of the spirit of the 1944 Act, and thereafter of what the Act allowed individual authorities to do. Such research as there was centred on the validity of selection tests. The accepted views of Burt and other psychologists began to be challenged, for example by Vernon, and more and more people began to doubt the fairness and desirability of selection at eleven. But of course this was by no means the same thing as establishing positively the validity of the comprehensive school idea.

Even the classic policy-making instrument of our time, the Advisory Committee Report, was not employed. Neither of the great post-war reports on secondary education, Crowther and Newsom, concerned itself with the issue. It was regarded as a political and social rather than an educational question. Such educational justification as there was came from individual writers like Robin Pedley or from reference to experience in the United States (and less frequently Russia) until there were British schools to see in action and to try to evaluate.

From this confluence of ideas and forces there emerged after a debate in the House of Commons in January 1965 a motion approving the efforts of local education authorities to 'reorganize secondary education on comprehensive lines which will preserve all that is valuable in grammar school education who now receive it and make it available to more children . . .' and calling for a declaration of national policy. In July came Circular 10/65 : 'The Secretary of State accordingly requests local education authorities, if they have not already done so, to prepare and submit to him plans for reorganizing secondary education in their areas on comprehensive lines.' These plans were to be submitted within one year : very great freedom was to be allowed over the type of organization adopted and over the time-scale of any changes.

It was inevitable that the legality of even this mild attempt at planning should be challenged. Some authorities questioned whether the Secretary of State had the power to require the submission of plans of this kind; others referred to 'government by ministerial pronouncement'; some refused to submit schemes at all. Section 68 empowered the Secretary of State to direct the activities of authorities who act 'unreasonably', but this had never been invoked and was in any case a weapon of doubtful value to compel an authority to implement a policy in which it did not believe and for which it would be financially entirely responsible. The only financial pressure possible was of a negative kind : Circular 13/66 a year later notified authorities that no new building could be approved unless it fitted in with secondary reorganization policy. In practice an authority had only to say that it would be willing to provide comprehensive education in schools built for the purpose but lacked the means to build them to find the Government in a poor position even to charge them with acting unreasonably.

Yet it was a step forward for those authorities that wished to reorganize. First they knew they had the backing of the Government in dealing with reluctant parents and teachers. Second it meant that consultation was possible between the Department's officers and local education officers on schemes of reorganization. This, incredibly, was something new.

The administrative operation described here is one in which an authority not having of its own initiative submitted plans for reorganization nevertheless accepted Government Policy. It is assumed for simplicity that the authority is a county borough : in counties there is the added complication of consulting with Divisional Executives about the provision needed for each area.

Circular 10/65

The operation begins then with Circular 10/65. Six types of comprehensive education are described. Authorities are told they may wish to have more than one kind and that types (iii) and (iv) are not fully comprehensive but are acceptable as interim solutions. They are then given opinions about the merits and problems of the six schemes: on sixth form colleges 'the issues have been sufficiently debated to justify a limited number of experiments'; on middle schools no more than 'a very small number of such proposals' would be approved (a restriction subsequently removed in the face of pressure from local education authorities). Voluntary schools are intended to be included in these schemes (though not necessarily following the same pattern as county schools), but beyond urging authorities to 'enter into discussions' with governors no advice is given about how to bring this about. On direct grant schools LEAs and governors are to 'consider ways of mounting and developing . . . co-operation in the context of the new policy of comprehensive education'. 'Close and genuine consultation' with teachers is urged once the principles and main outline of a possible plan have been formulated. Parents cannot be consulted but they are to be informed fully and authoritatively of the plans as early as possible. Plans are to be in two stages (i) long-term proposals and (ii) detailed proposals for a three year period from September 1967.

The machinery for conducting the exercise will probably first be set up by an item on the agenda of an early sub-committee meeting. Let us say the decision is (*a*) to concentrate on the county school problem first and (*b*) to set up a working party to consider ways and means and in due course to prepare a scheme or schemes of reorganization. The committee also have to decide on the composition of the working party: so many members of the education committee and so many teachers; or so many members of the education committee with power to consult teachers' associations; or so many teachers to prepare a scheme together with the education officer for members' consideration; or a mixed group of members, teachers and officers. The possible variations are endless. There are also many methods of procedure but usually the rhythm will begin with the production of reports by the education officer for consideration by the working party.

It will be a rare and happy chance if the particular variety of secondary organization desired coincides with the practical possibilities of the buildings. In practice the educational merits of an

97

orthodox eleven-eighteen comprehensive system may have to be set aside if the authority does not have a sufficient number of grammar and modern school buildings so close together that they can be regarded as complete units. There is a danger that any scheme will start from the stock of buildings available and rationalize the philosophy to match : this is inevitable when the proposal is to reorganize by making use of existing buildings. This more than any other aspect of reorganization has worried conscientious education officers and teachers.

The chance to ensure that educational considerations come first may arise from widening the scope of the enquiry—a possibility that the country owes to the West Riding Authority and its Chief Education Officer, Sir Alec Clegg, as much as to anyone. Incisive and persistent probing of the logic, long assumed but never tested, of transfer at eleven led in the end to a surprising consensus—that a later age, twelve or thirteen, would be better. And many authorities found that a survey of the whole range of educational buildings and organization gave them more scope to strike a balance rather less favourable to logistics and more to educational philosophy. Thus the middle school idea and the notion of junior colleges began to flourish.

Whatever scheme is chosen it will not emerge without a lot of argument. Vested interests—whether in the shape of pet theories or prejudices of a more tangible kind—are almost certain to emerge. The enquiry will be conducted honestly in a spirit of seeking after truth, no doubt, but there is no point in pretending that personal issues may not also be at stake. This may diminish somewhat the value of consultation with teachers, especially if an attempt is made to combine working out schemes with discussion of their impact on teachers' professional expectations. Both are legitimate objects of consultation, but they are better handled separately. Nevertheless the education officer will always have in the forefront of his mind that a scheme with the backing of the teachers' associations is more likely to work than one that is opposed. Conversely he will advise his committee to think twice about any scheme that all the teachers' associations condemn.

Apart from the special position of teachers, the stage of consultation is perhaps the trickiest of a very tricky operation. How far, and how, should an authority proceed before seeking the views of those concerned who are not members of the LEA? If the working party is not primarily a consultative body but a means of producing ideas it should normally be the main source of schemes to be considered by the education committee. If its function is consultative the education officer will probably have the job of submitting his own schemes first to a sub-committee of the authority and then to the working party for their comments. Even if the terms of reference are clear there may be clashes: if they are not the clashes will be worse.

The education officer must advise the committee on the right moment for discussion with the teachers' associations. Too soon and it may be a waste of time: too late and opposition to a *fait accompli* may cloud any merits the scheme may have. Another dilemma arises from the committee structure. Should their representatives discuss with the teachers a scheme that has not been approved by the committee? Can they legally do so since the scheme has no status until it has been before the committee? On the other hand the value of consultation will be diminished if it takes place after a decision has been made. One answer is for the committee to authorize its representatives to discuss schemes before submitting them for approval.

There comes a moment when the debate moves from general principles to consideration of particular schools. At this point the governors will wish to know what is being proposed. Because this widens the scope of consultation substantially it is more practical to think in terms of doing this only after education committee approval. This is the time, too, to consult the heads of the schools affected and for them to inform their staffs. As teachers they will be represented by their associations in the main stream of consultation, but their own personal problems are a matter for separate discussion.

The education officer also has to choose carefully the time to start informal discussions with the DES. The local HMI may have been in the picture confidentially from the start but when what looks like a possible scheme emerges the Department's view may be a decisive factor. If it is known, for instance, that the Department does not favour a particular approach the committee should at least know that before they commit themselves to it.

It would be surprising if the public were not taking a lively interest in all this, particularly if there is disagreement. How can the LEA keep them informed, reassure them and take account of their views? Very few of the public are likely to be well-informed on the educational issues; concern for their children tends to colour their views; sheer weight of numbers precludes anything but the most superficial discussion of the issues. The parents of children already at school are the ones most immediately concerned and the heads of the schools affected are the obvious people to keep them informed. Heads of secondary schools may find it difficult to give objective advice in these circumstances—though most of them do it surprisingly well. Public meetings or internal school meetings attended by a senior education officer may be useful. It is important to keep the heads of primary schools informed—and to consult them—about the progress of discussion on reorganization. If this is done then they in turn can keep the parents in touch and help to answer their queries and allay their fears.

Section 13 of the 1944 Act requires publication of notices when schools are to be reorganized. This has to be thought of as something more than a formal legal requirement. All parents should be informed, as part of the programme of information and advice, of the purpose and timing of this operation. Of course by this time the education committee will have made their decision, but this is by no means irrevocable. There is nothing worse than the sudden shock of a starkly worded official notice without previous warning.

Once the local decision is made the education officer will turn his attention to practical and psychological problems. Obviously he cannot proceed with the arrangements until he has the Secretary of State's decision but he will need the breathing space between submission and answer to make his plans. Some of the main issues will have been settled in advance. Salary protection to those affected is now a matter of national agreement, but there are many side issues and the actual salary is only one factor. Equally important to most teachers is status : reorganization of many small schools into fewer large ones means fewer headships. The method of filling the new posts has to be settled; so is the treatment of those not appointed to them. Some authorities have tried to fill all the new posts from the staffs of the schools incorporated in the new comprehensives; others have advertised all posts within the authority's service; some have even gone outside. Whatever is decided will have been discussed at length with the teachers' associations so that even if they do not agree at least they have had a chance to put their point of view. Thereafter there is need for some machinery—perhaps a meeting at each school—for anyone involved to find out the details as they affect him.

Schemes of staffing, special allowances, equipment and of course building for the new schools will need to be put in hand. It is an exercise calling for co-ordination and skill and it may well have to be performed against the clock. Network analysis of the component parts may help to match the quality of implementation to that of the scheme.

It is the education officer's particular responsibility to see that morale is high, in his own staff, who may well have unprecedented and thankless burdens, and in the schools, where insecurity can easily transmit itself to the pupils and their work. Even if all goes well this is difficult to achieve and of course in the atmosphere of political tension frequently found it can be almost impossible. In the end the quality of the scheme is the decisive factor. If it is a good one then the chances are that in the end it will be accepted by everyone concerned and can really become the exciting challenge that is talked about so much but less frequently achieved.

Scarcely any authority has been able to produce satisfactory reorganization schemes including the voluntary and direct grant schools in their area. For the voluntary schools, even if their sponsors are willing to contemplate changes, the extra cost of adapting schools perhaps only recently completed may be a daunting if not impossible prospect. Within these limits the philosophy and influence of the church authorities can be decisive and the earlier discussions with them can begin the better. Perhaps they may be associated, as observers, with negotiations over county school reorganization so as to familiarize them with the issues. Clearly if at all possible similar schemes should be adopted for county and voluntary schools, but the financial resources to help to bring this about are in the hands of the Government not the local authorities.

With direct grant schools the position is even more difficult. Usually their traditions are quite other than the philosophy of the comprehensive schools. They may be highly selective and may see the prospect of becoming still more so if the rest of the schools in the area become comprehensive. Even if they are willing to take part in a reorganization scheme it is hard to see how a three- or four-form entry school can widen the academic range of its intake without losing some of its quality. Transfer at thirteen does offer some possibility of a bigger form-entry and thus of a wider range of studies; there may also be prospects of transfer into the sixth form.

For any widespread prospects of change in all types of school the central government would need to take action both legislatory and financial. Thus any movement towards comprehensive education is likely to be gradual. Current legislation is concerned mainly with requiring authorities to submit proposals. It seems likely therefore that education officers will have to contend with schemes of reorganization for many years to come.

Characteristic elements

The two-way process is evident in both the examples chosen: the correct balance between projecting ideas and responding to external pressures is largely a matter at first of intuition and later of judgement based on experience. Most of the other characteristic elements of educational administration can be seen in the processes that have been described. They apply both to the texture of administration (the techniques used) and to its structure (the objectives and attitudes it embodies).

Amongst the techniques we can distinguish three separate but related activities. First, initiating ideas. This is usually more associated with field-workers than administrators, but in our system the education officer is in a unique position. The DES is mainly concerned with control, whereas the LEAs own the schools and determine the educational pattern of their area, so that development is largely in their hands. The ideas may come in the dead of night as a result of black coffee and sheer abstract thought, but the education officer's characteristic insight is the result of apparently chance confrontations, more like catching a butterfly than building a philosophy. In discussion there may be a flash of recognition, a half-hint or a by-product recalled and mulled over later.

The second process is gathering and presenting information. This is discussed in a later chapter, so all that needs to be said here is that even the best ideas may founder if this process is skimped or neglected. The third technique, assessing and judging, is mainstream administration, the classical function. The ideas of colleagues, headmasters' schemes, applications for grants—all in their own way call for the exercise of judgement.

So far as the projection of objectives and attitudes is concerned, planning and budgeting are the two key words. As we have seen we have to be cautious about using the word planning in the education officer's work. Those who hold the controls must have the main responsibility for planning, and this means the DES. The possibilities are at longest middle-term: development plans, network analysis, building programmes. Since much long-term planning is crippled by the uncertain and pragmatic temper of our particular brand of democratic government middle and short-term planning becomes even more vital. And in this context planning includes not only preparing schemes but adopting an organized approach to any activity about which it is possible to take careful thought in advance.

In this category comes budgeting. This is a crucial instrument of planning in any organization, and in public authorities, which pioneered the technique, it is a dominant feature. Chapter 10 deals with education budgeting in more detail: here the point to be made is that the education officer has to see the budget as an aspect of planning policy not merely as a financial record.

In all of these activities the initiative is with the administrator. But there are important ways in which administration is a response, not initiation. Thus decision-making usually becomes necessary as a result of a combination of circumstances capable of different ways of resolution. Two hazards in education are the relative absence of black-and-white issues and the multiplicity of people who may need to be consulted before a decision can be made. The result may be atrophy of the decision-making faculty. Much of the uncertainty felt by teachers and parents in contact with an education authority stems from the state of suspended judgement that seems to pervade the system. The education officer is the prisoner not the architect of the system but he can do two things: first explain to everyone concerned just what the obstacles to reaching a decision are, and second make sure that the decisions that do fall within his power are quickly made and implemented.

Another responsive activity is day-to-day administration. This not very helpful phrase is understood by administrators but perhaps merely accepted by others. Probably the impression it creates—of telephones ringing, letters being answered, drafts being read, interviews and committees being held—is as good a way as any of describing what must be to most junior administrators and some of their seniors their main occupation. To handle this side of the work efficiently is an achievement in itself and to say that it is here that judicious delegation can be most helpful is not to minimize its importance.

Embedded in the notion are a number of important elements: for example, that of the education officer as provider not planner, and of the public service as a response to public need. An aspect that should be mentioned specifically is trouble-shooting, if only because there are times when the education officer feels that he only comes into the picture when there is trouble. The more senior he becomes the stronger the feeling grows, and he may need to remind himself how valuable his function is in this situation. Those closely concerned in an incident are those most likely to be emotionally involved—for instance in a clash of wills between a head and a parent—and the administrator can often help because no personal feelings arise, he does not feel his authority threatened or his liberty infringed. This does not mean he can be icily detached or loftily unmoved, but rather that he is free to direct his sympathy into constructive channels.

There is an important sense in which all administrative activities are responses : none of them would happen at all but for the need to solve certain problems. So while bearing in mind the considerable initiatives open to the administrator we can perhaps accept as the most revealing single phrase to sum it up that it is essentially a problem-solving activity. This is the angle from which it will be considered in the next two chapters.

7

Basic issues

To describe administration as a problem-solving activity is to reveal its proper limitations : it is not philosophy, nor even policy-making. Yet as a description of the work of the best education officers it is too restrictive. There is another dimension, that of concern.

There is no process in educational administration that can be done completely satisfactorily unless those with responsibility for it care deeply about the fundamental purposes of the service. So we must begin consideration of the problems that present themselves for solution with the basic issues. The most basic of all is how to ensure that every child has equality of opportunity to take advantage of the education offered.

Part of the difficulty of getting to grips with this problem is understanding the question. Almost everyone agrees that equality of opportunity is the aim, but almost no one agrees what it means. It is a matter of values, so that in a democracy there can be no definitive standards. In a democracy, too, there is always an uneasy balance between the individual's rights and the needs of society, and the balance shifts according to the changing circumstances of the national economy, changing moral attitudes and growing knowledge.

Free secondary education for all seemed a great advance in 1944 and much of the argument about equal opportunity since has centred on whether this means the same secondary school for all. Yet the evidence grows that for many children this is a question of marginal relevance : the dice are loaded against them before they even start at primary school. And to remove the barrier of poverty is not enough to ensure an equal chance.

The focus of attention has shifted from economics to the home itself: the quality of housing; parental occupation and its expectations; the family's social and cultural horizons; the mother's efficiency; the strong, intangible influences of the parents' standards whatever their theoretical aspirations for their children.

The conflict of opinion covers a good deal of ground. Does the country's future depend on using scarce resources to let the able and willing to come to the fore? Or is there more to be said economically and politically as well as morally for seeking out and using the hidden reservoir of talent that successive reports on education have described? Are there undesirable overtones of superiority and *Brave New World* in trying to reduce the influence of working-class parents, however inadequate, on their own children? On the other hand is it fair to leave a child's future in the hands of uninterested or hostile parents?

These unanswered questions run like a thread through the education service. The education officer is not concerned with them in the abstract or in full. He has to try to work towards a solution to such particular aspects as his job brings to light, working on inadequate information within a framework of regular national and local political change and in a climate of uncertain public opinion.

His attitude to the organization of secondary education may be written off by some because it is not based on controlled experiment and research over a long period. Yet, given the limited impact of research on either politicians or teachers and the sheer impossibility of measuring the unfathomable, he turns to the evidence of his daily work and experience as the basis of the advice he gives. And he often has to give advice whether he feels the time is ripe or not. His attitude towards the recruitment of teachers may lean towards putting the best teachers in the most favoured schools, or he may try to steer promising teachers into areas of greatest social need. Either way he has to make a decision and whichever it is, it is governed by reality: he risks losing staff or depriving children or both. It is in questions such as these that the link between administrative action and the quality of education is closest.

So he must seek answers where he can. First he might look within himself. Parental attitudes are a two-way thing, and even in families where there is willingness to do the best for the children there are barriers within the service that at best dampen enthusiasm and at worst set up hostile reactions. There is an inescapable middle-class aura about the system: one that may suggest a remoteness, an insulation from reality, and at the same time induce inferiority feelings. Schools, especially big new ones, some teachers, and most education offices may induce reactions that shut some people out from the advice and information they need. Brian Jackson and Dennis Marsden's *Education and the Working Class* has a revealing passage about parents seeking help in choosing a secondary school. First they try with varying success the heads of the primary schools and their teachers. A few of them visit the education office and retire baffled at the offhand bureaucracy of the junior staff they manage to see: they had imagined a personal chat with the CEO himself. In one case a forceful councillor insists on Pike, the Education Officer, making an appointment. It is a sad picture.

Of course even in a small office Pike cannot possibly see every parent personally. Indeed if his staff are properly trained they might do better by seeing subordinates, who are likely to know more about the situation than Pike himself. But the important thing is the atmosphere generated throughout the office, and that is the responsibility of the CEO personally. It is the staff on the perimeter walls who convey the impression to the public outside of what an office is like. Reception staff, telephone operators and juniors manning counters are key people who need to be specially chosen and properly briefed.

It is not always easy to create the right atmosphere in vast Victorian buildings or modern plate-glass palaces. Experiments have been tried with 'education shops', smaller, informal kiosks where questions can be asked and answered without embarrassment. But old habits die hard, and they have not been notably successful. Working class parents may simply be too inarticulate to handle a transaction of this kind. Eventually an enlargement of the scope and size of the education welfare service may make more progress, by taking advice to the home.

The sociologists have pointed out other ways in which working class attitudes may conflict with those of the school situation. The group or the gang is a co-operative enterprise natural to those needing to band together for strength. Most schools encourage individual striving and effort corresponding more closely with the middle class, individualistic ethic of free enterprise. W. J. H. Sprott in *Human Groups* says: 'The advantages of co-operation are, it may be argued, just what we should expect: the characteristics we think of as "team spirit" are present. We might, however ask ourselves whether educationalists make enough use of the principles enunciated in formidable detail by Deutsch. Do we perhaps use individual competition too much?'

But in a democracy the education service generally follows the patterns and values of society : it cannot overtly change them on the bigger issues. Any school operating on co-operative rather than competitive lines will tend to plough a lonely furrow and to be under-valued by employers and influential parents. Schools are urged more and more to look outward, to close the gap between the classroom and the outside world. If this happens in contemporary society they become more competitive, not less.

It looks, then, as though true equality of opportunity can only come from changes in society that reduce inequalities in social conditions and attitudes. Even the neighbourhood comprehensive school tends to be only as good as its neighbourhood allows.

Positive discrimination

'Equality has an appealing ring, discrimination has not.' The Plowden Report pointed out the inadequacy of provision that is merely equal as a means of giving equal opportunity to the underprivileged. The national survey in 1964, which strongly influenced the Report, suggested that of three variables in a child's education—parental attitudes, home environment and the quality of the school—the first carried most weight. The Report makes many practical suggestions for bringing parents into the scheme of things, particularly those not normally involved : the school, it says should go out to the parent rather than waiting for him to come to it. The main responsibility for this rests with the teachers, though encouragement from the office would do no harm.

Where the education officer comes in is with the radical proposal, cutting deep into traditions and assumptions, of positive discrimination. There is a vicious circle of deprivation—children from poor districts tend to have the worst school buildings which tend to attract fewer teachers—which should be reversed. Authorities are urged to compensate for poor environment by giving the children a better education than that offered in good districts : extra teachers with higher salaries, extra equipment and priority in schemes for new and improved buildings, educational priority areas.

It is interesting that the phrase Educational Priority Areas quickly caught on and was duly awarded its set of initials EPA, to prove that it had arrived. The justice of turning attention to the primary schools and especially those in poor areas was readily accepted. Yet the full implications were not, and positive discrimination had a cautious reception.

As the Report said, the idea of fair shares for all is more deeply rooted in local than central government. This is not surprising : closely knit areas with more immediate control by elected members representing particular districts tend to produce allocation systems of a simple kind. Education officers need to be cautious in applying any discriminatory influence : members even more so.

But it is not merely locally, but nationally that people have found it hard to accept the full rigour of the Plowden argument. Most of the key decisions are in fact for the central government : extra teachers for the EPA schools means a relaxation of the quota system; extra allowances can only come from the Burnham Committee; building programmes are nationally operated. Ventures like the Urban programme, offering specific grants for educational and social improvement, would need to be expanded considerably to come anywhere near the Plowden ideal. Meanwhile progress is likely to be made gradually, erratically and unsystematically : in whichever small ways chance allows.

Priorities

The Plowden Committee determined its priorities according to criteria that were lucidly and logically expressed and based on the same social and educational premises as the 1944 Act itself. The depth of social concern and psychological insight is greater but the principles are the same. Within the primary sector—which it shows to be both neglected and essential to later educational development —it outlines a programme for ten years of advance : the EPAs; the introduction of teachers' aides inside as well as outside the classroom; improving bad buildings; extending nursery education and changing the traditional age ranges of primary schools.

But the problem of priorities within the education service extends beyond the primary sector, and other factors than educational and social ones come into the reckoning. As long ago as 1945 an American, Harold F. Clark, analysed the reasons for the relative poverty and affluence of ten countries. He showed that 'education raised the level of production of a people. The case of a country such as Denmark provides striking proof over a long period of time. Here we have a country that one hundred years ago was poor and had few resources. It increased its technical training and a high income has resulted. There's every reason to think that the same result would follow in the rest of the world if education were increased.' Later evidence has supported this conclusion and education as an investment is now a commonplace of economic thinking. So reference to untapped resources in other educational Reports—Crowther, Newsom, Robbins—have been added to the purely social considerations as an argument for developing certain sectors of education.

This raises two questions that have to be answered—somehow—by a nation with limited resources. How much can be spent on investment in education as distinct from other aspects of society; and within education, which sector gives the best return on investment? The answers to these questions do not come easily in a democracy : there is no authoritative source from which they can spring. So these major issues have only ever been resolved provisionally, tentatively and subject to revision. And local decisions on priorities can be no more than marginal and temporary : progress tends to be unplanned because there is a danger of built-in obsolescence if sights are set too far in the distance.

Priorities over a five year period are perhaps as much as can sensibly be determined; the annual review at the time of the revenue estimates or submission of building programmes is even more realistic. Within these limits the notion of priorities is vital to local administration. Comparison of the merits of compelling projects within a limited budget is a crucial process. The criteria used for solving this recurring problem are not fixed : they arise as occasion demands from the inter-relation of philosophy and administrative skill.

Cost-effective planning

When a long-term process like education is subject to short term political decision and financial control the opportunities for planning are limited, particularly planning in terms of value for money. There are difficulties, too, in trying to measure the quality of educational output in order to try to relate it to costs. What criteria are there? Examination results are part, but only part, of the story. The production of different types of skilled manpower is associated more with countries with specific, controlled manpower targets, where efficiency outweighs democracy in the national scales. Traditionally English education is concerned with other, less tangible aims, and there is concern to free the schools from external pressures, from examinations and from industry.

How can there be cost-effective planning then? The ancillary branches, such as school meals and supplies can clearly be treated in the same way as any other branch of industry: as can head-quarters staffing. But what about the main fabric of the service where the biggest costs arise? The local education officer cannot be expected to perform miracles when the whole system points him in another direction. Yet he can, with patience and resource, take a few halting steps forward.

A lot will depend on the accounting system and the way the treasurer uses it. The traditional purpose of local authority accounts has been to guard against dishonesty: this and the fact that public services are not expected to make a profit has tended to obscure the real potentialities of positive cost accounting. Never-theless, the budget is itself a useful planning tool, and analysis of its components can be developed. So can the study of variations from the estimates. Unit-costing is a fairly well-developed technique in local government and this at least gives a quantitative measurement —so much per child—as a basis for comparison with other authorities.

But beyond this the picture may grow dim. Commitment account-ing—giving up-to-date information on spending trends before the final accounts are received—is not common, for reasons not apparent to the layman. Standard costs (computed for a particular operation, regarded temporarily as actual costs and compared later with true costs) arc rare. Output or programme-planning budgeting can make a tremendous contribution if the imaginative and technical leap can be made.

In his own sphere the education officer will look to matters not related to technical mysteries. The process is unlikely to be as precise and scientific as some would have it, but there can never be accurate measurement of impalpable educational values. It will probably amount to no more than following through certain pointers as they arise, pointers from different directions which seem to lead to the same spot. We have already noticed that what makes educa-tional sense may often make economic sense. For instance tiny sixth form groups are not only costly in staffing but frequently fail to give the stimulus to a pupil that he would get from a larger group. And again habitual spending—the unreflecting inclusion of items year by year in the estimates—is not merely bad economics, but may indicate insufficient thought about the changing needs of changing times.

Resources for learning

Habitual spending is the result of habitual thinking. The pressures of routine procedures and sheer weight of events disguise the need for analysis of existing practices. Inflation of costs can arise without corresponding benefits in terms of results. Economists have pointed out that education costs have risen spectacularly since the war compared with say, the Health Service: yet the Health Service has achieved a dramatic increase in work. We have referred already to the difficulty of measuring output in education, and to the difficulty (and perhaps the danger) of trying to achieve sheer efficiency in an essentially democratic service. Nevertheless after a period of great expansion there is likely to be a drop in the rate of growth of money available for education. So more intensive use of existing resources will be needed.

This is perhaps the side of education most in need of research: significantly it is left to the Nuffield Foundation to sponsor the first enquiry of any substance. The 'Resources for Learning' project could make an outstanding contribution to educational advance. It is an area of myths, sacred cows, half-truths and platitudes and there is a real danger that brief comments may add to them. What is needed is organized examination of assumptions not hunches or prejudices. Yet the problem exists now, and whatever the findings of the Nuffield Project there will be no easy answers handed down on tablets from the mountain top. There is a place, too, for enquiry that is local, individual and sustained.

The biggest cost is on teachers' salaries so the enquiry must centre on the use made of scarce teaching staff. It can be shown that teachers' salaries are a lower proportion of education costs than before the war though the salary scales themselves have increased considerably. Other industries have done better still in reducing the labour cost-fraction but education's relatively slow progress reflects the essentially personal nature of the teaching process as at present conceived. Many of the questions now being asked are expressions of doubt about whether it really needs to be quite so personal.

Can machines help? Much more is spent on equipment than in the past, largely because the approach to teaching has changed— from chalk and talk through demonstration to learning by doing— and because the range of studies has increased. But many of the advocates of teaching machines are more interested in using them to replace, not supplement, some of the teacher's functions.

Two distinct types of machine are being developed each with quite different potentialities. One is the approach through mass media, notably television: the other is individual self-instruction by language laboratories and teaching machines. The argument for the mass media is that one teacher can give lessons to many more children than by class-teaching. One argument for the teaching machine is to supply what is conspicuously absent from the mass media, reinforcement and opportunity for questioning. Teachers would always be needed as counsellors even if the machines could handle the whole range of teaching—which they cannot by any means yet do—and in large numbers as programme planners : a link is needed between the mass presentation and the individual project. Such research as there has been suggests that the use of teachers for small tutorial groups, not class-teaching, is the vital factor in weighing the balance between economic and uneconomic use of staff resources. Enormous savings would have to be made in the mass presentation side to compensate for this. So in the foreseeable future it seems unlikely that machinery can make any impact on the numbers of teachers needed.

Can we conceive of teaching machines so sophisticated that they could in fact rise above the level of teaching aids? Sir Alec Clegg has provided most people's answer :

> A man came to sell me one—a teaching machine. I said,
> 'Does it do subject and predicate and long division?' He
> looked at me scornfully and said, 'It does creative English,
> blowing bubbles and all that, and it does Nuffield science and
> mathematics.' I then said, 'Does it do goodness, truth and
> beauty?' and he said, 'It'll do all that and on the Mark IV
> there are two dummy knobs for sweetness and light which
> you can have added at £300 apiece.'
> And then I said, 'What about Plowden aspiration?' and he
> countered, 'We've thought of that and every time the
> pupil gets anything right a mechanical hand shoots out, pats
> him on the back and says, "Well done, Charlie".' And then
> I woke up and it dawned on me that I should get about
> as much encouragement from being patted on the back by a
> computer as I should ecstasy from embracing one, no
> matter how cunningly it was contrived.

The economic advantages must for the present be sought in less dramatic but more subtle form. Closed-circuit television can not only provide first-class instruction and stimulate teachers to develop skills to match the power of the medium, it can make good deficiencies in specialist subjects. For example, in teaching French to primary school children it may be difficult to find enough teachers with good enough accents to provide conversation practice : this can be done very satisfactorily by television. The Open University could transform the possibilities of adult education by reaching more people cheaply.

But as a local exercise the enquiry into resources for learning is likely to be concerned with other things than machinery. Some of these—team teaching and the use of skilled ancillaries for lesser classroom tasks—will depend on the delicate processes of negotiation with teachers and the passage of time. Others may be quicker in coming. For example there might be more intensive use of school and college buildings. The extension of the school day for older pupils might be achieved by providing homework and recreational facilities in charge of a limited number of supervisory staff, who need not be teachers. Under-use of equipment might be avoided by sharing; specialist accommodation or even teaching could be shared between schools; colleges of further education could be used for special day-release sessions for school children to enlarge their range of choice of subject; co-operation between schools at sixth form level could help in the same way. The implications of time-tabling on staffing are not always fully understood: courses and seminars on the relationship between curriculum, the timetable and staffing could be of immense value.

Devolution of responsibility

In education there are no clear sources of power from which changes can spring. The system is so complex and so fluid that it would be pointless to seek efficiency through trying to bring control into as few hands as possible. The principle of democracy is to bring the power to control as near as possible to those affected by it. To reconcile this with efficiency means devolving responsibility to those who operate the service.

Responsibility does not mean the same as power. The difference explains why administrators intent on devolution do not always find it so easy. Heads of schools, for instance, may not leap eagerly at proposals for handing them greater freedom to control their own affairs. Perhaps they may sometimes suspect that there is a catch in it. And of course there is. Devolving responsibility associates the one exercising it with the decisions and this may bring unpopularity and anxiety.

The award of above-scale allowances for heads of departments in schools is the responsibility of the LEA: they have discretion within the general guidance of the Burnham reports. They can if they wish decide each case on its merits, considering applications

114

from heads for establishing or regrading certain posts. Or they can set aside a sum of money appropriate to the size of the schools and leave it to the head to decide how it is shared out. This gives more freedom to the person best fitted to exercise it. What are the objections?

First, the notion of managing within agreed limits is a relatively new one in education. Public service tradition in general has a strong element of trying to prise out as much as possible from the Treasury. Broad discretion and global sums can make it more difficult to justify increases than arguing particular cases. Second, personal relations with the staff may be easier if it is thought that decisions over increased allowances are made at headquarters rather than by the head.

Yet responsibility such as this is essential if we are to make sense of the system. The alternative is constant tension, constant dissatisfaction, the feeling that 'they' have to solve all the problems by waving a magic wand. Problem-solving, in conditions of limited resources in a democratic framework, has to be a co-operative venture.

Parts of the whole

These few examples have been used to underline the fundamental quality—caring—that the education officer must apply, if he applies nothing else, to the problems he seeks to solve. The basic issues are, above all, about people. Educational administration has to turn this concern into practical benefit and to do so as efficiently and economically as possible. Equality of opportunity, positive discrimination, priorities, cost-effective planning and resources for learning are issues that lead naturally one from the other : they cannot be considered separately. And devolution of responsibility is the way in which, the priorities once settled, efficiency can be reconciled with the democratic basis of the education service.

These problems are hard enough on their own. They are intractable to the point of impossibility when they have to be considered together, each complicating the situation for the others. But there is an added source of trouble for the education officer. For, of course, they do not arise as separate and easily detectable philosophical issues but as aspects, often apparently incidental, of day-to-day administration. In the next chapter we look more closely at some of the specific problems, to illustrate their range and nature.

8

Problems in practice

A quick scamper through issues that could each provide a subject for a book in themselves is a hazardous enterprise. Compression brings distortion: comment invites expert demolition. So it had better be made clear that there is no pretence at suggesting solutions to these resounding questions. Even when they are considered fully these issues will always be difficult: any answers are likely to be tentative, applicable only at one time, palliative, the lesser of two evils.

Here the purpose is in any event strictly limited: to show something of the range and nature of problems in educational administration. It is a necessary reminder at this point, for in turning to look at ways in which fundamental problems show themselves in practice, the references to the problems themselves will become even briefer and more perfunctory. For once—only for once and only for this purpose—the administrative side is more important than the issues.

Problems of organization

Ages of transfer

No one need be surprised that this should be a problem. It is another example of the difficulties of objective research, planning and decision-making in a democratic service. Do we have to wait until everybody agrees before making a change? At what stage and on what basis can the Secretary of State make a pronouncement? How far is it a national issue and how far a matter of local discretion? Clearly there is much to be said in our increasingly mobile society for a uniform system of ages and stages throughout the country. There is, however, an even more fundamental question: how far is it desirable to have standard ages of transfer at all. Can it not be a matter for individual decision based on the child's stage of development?

The recommendations of the Plowden report could be used to resolve the dilemma. They would give a national policy for a locally determined framework aimed at considering the needs of individuals. Nursery education, part-time for most and full-time for some, would interlock with starting in the first primary school, where the normal starting time in the September after the child's fifth birthday would allow part-time schooling up to the age of six. There would be flexibility in the age of transfer from first to middle school round about the age of eight. It is at the next stage—transfer to secondary school—that accepting the recommendations would become harder for the Government.

The proposal is to have transfer at twelve plus. In relaxing the restrictions on local experiments with transfer at other ages than eleven the national voice has perhaps spoken as loudly as it can. In order to bring about a change there would need to be first a strong upsurge of educational and public support and second direct financial incentives to the local authorities to help them make the change. The organizational questions raised in the Plowden Report are likely to remain local ones, for the education officer and his committee.

Types of secondary education

The same remains substantially true of the organization of secondary education even though there has been a declaration of government policy. The Secretary of State has either to convince all authorities of the wisdom and justice of his policy or seek to control and develop through finance. Without this he is left with the negative control of excluding from building programmes projects that do not fit in with comprehensive planning. Unless there is some change in this financial relationship there are likely to be many more varieties of secondary school than even the wide range mentioned in Circular 10/65.

The classical comprehensive school is for children from eleven to eighteen or nineteen, but authorities wishing to use existing buildings find them too small to admit an adequate number of form-entries to cover the full ability range. Consequently it may be difficult to decide whether proposals to vary the age-range are based on educational factors or the promptings of logistics. This is perhaps one of the strongest arguments for recruiting education officers from committed educationists. In an ideal world the policy would come first and the school would be built later but life is not like that.

There are doubts too about the desirability of the large comprehensive school generally thought to be needed to build up a convincing sixth form. Some authorities are turning their attention, therefore, to secondary schools from eleven (or more likely twelve) to sixteen followed by junior colleges : pooling the resources of expert staff, reducing the age range and providing a taste of the adult world at the right age. Again it may be that such a plan will fit existing buildings better than other schemes and any solutions will find it hard to escape the charge of administrative convenience.

The problem, difficult enough in itself, is a small-scale version of the general one of reform in a developed society : it always has to start from an existing situation and, together with the hazard that the change may not in any event be an improvement, there is the additional difficulty of trying to use what exists in a new way.

Teacher supply

Whatever the organization the problems of recruitment and distribution of teachers persist : indeed they are intensified when uncertainty about the future makes teachers try to steer clear of certain authorities and certain types of school. Within an authority the quota must be observed if possible : the falling population of big cities and the shifts of population between primary and secondary sectors make it harder to achieve.

The quota system introduced in 1956 was intended to arrest the uncontrolled drift of teachers to areas of the country which for social climatic and aesthetic reasons have a natural attraction for teachers. This it has done, though it has not gone as far as some would like in equalizing staff-pupil ratios, and it is unfortunate to say the least that industrial cities with declining populations should have had to reduce their establishment of teachers at the very time when the notion of positive discrimination to compensate for poor social environment was emerging.

County and County Borough problems are somewhat different.

The counties may have uneconomic small schools in places to which it is difficult to attract staff. Yet the big industrial cities with decaying centres face the constant problem of recruiting and retaining teachers in down-town schools. Many teachers, even if they begin their service in these districts, are attracted to posts in the suburbs—where of course they tend to live. A few are dedicated to the service of under-privileged children : some perhaps stay too long in inner area schools where the limitations and environment can in time blunt the keen edge of imaginative enthusiasm.

Links between sectors of education

The division of the education service into three stages is a convenient and necessary administrative device, but it has its drawbacks. Links between primary and secondary schools and between schools and colleges of further education are surprisingly weak in some authorities. Relationships between methods of teaching are left largely to chance : follow-up of pupils' progress and advice on special needs of individuals are too rare. Organized regular meetings between heads and assistant teachers and well-designed record cards can help.

At school-leaving stage the need for liaison is just as great : on admission standards for courses at further education colleges; on avoiding overlapping provision in fifth and sixth forms and in colleges; on planning new further education courses. Heads of secondary schools may sometimes serve on college governing bodies. Again regular meetings between heads of departments, perhaps associated on some occasions with youth employment officers and careers teachers, can improve working relationships.

Development and control in further education

We have discussed earlier some of the problems in further education. Clearly in such a complex, essentially voluntary system growth and response to external stimuli are likely to play a major part in determining the shape of the system. Clearly too, technical colleges, youth and community services and adult education are more likely to differ radically from one area to another than the schools. The needs of rural and urban communities are very different and call for different kinds of approach. Yet whatever the local circumstances, the voluntary nature of this sector means that patterns of development and control are needed, different from those in the schools.

In most further education institutions there is a fairly direct relationship between the number of students and the level of courses and the salary of the staff. There are no predetermined limits to the potential number of students or courses as in the school situation. So stimulation is only rarely necessary: more often the need is for control. The basic situation is one in which the principal proposes additional courses and various other agencies decide whether or not it can go forward.

Much of the responsibility for these decisions rests with education officers, in direct and indirect ways. For evening institute and adult education courses the decision is usually made administratively according to the number of students. At the other end of the scale, many other agencies are involved in approval of advanced courses— the DES, the Regional Advisory Council, perhaps the CNAA. Other courses are normally the responsibility of the governors, advised by the principal and the education officer, and subject to approval of the education committee.

At all levels finance plays an important part. Students are still charged fees in further education (though firms pay many part-time fees for their employees and LEAs cover most full-time fees by way of grants) and this can be a source of income. The level of fees is normally discussed regionally though they are a matter for local discretion: invariably they cover only a small part of the cost of the course. Further education crosses local boundaries and when a student from one area goes to college in another the providing authority can claim seven-eighths of the cost from the sending authority. Urban authorities can often look to a considerable income to offset their costs since they tend to serve a wide area. The cost of advanced courses is reimbursed from the pool collected from all authorities.

In an essentially competitive system control is clearly needed. At advanced level the Regional Staff Inspector of the DES is advised by the Regional Council: further down it is a matter for the authorities themselves. It cannot be said to be very severe at either level. The national rise and fall of demand in some fields as industries wax and wane is one reason; another is the reluctance of authorities to close down courses when staff and equipment are already there; a third is the inflationary nature of the financial arrangements which involve one authority providing and other authorities helping to pay. The Pilkington Report revealed widespread under-use of resources and recommended more stringent standards. It is at the planning stage when control is most needed: authorities need to work together to avoid overlap.

120

Problems of quality

Reading methods

Nothing is more fundamental to the education system than that children should be taught to read well. Should we be glad or sorry then that this vital matter is left almost entirely to the discretion of the teacher who happens to be taking the class to which the child is admitted? We have no choice, since there is no accepted method of teaching reading. There has of course been voluminous research since the middle of the nineteenth century and the research has made more impact on teaching methods than in most subjects. We have made a good deal of progress: for instance hardly anyone would now begin teaching reading by teaching the alphabet. Yet it is possible for a young teacher to emerge from a college which favours one method to serve in a school where the head favours another and to be visited by an adviser who is enthusiastic about a third.

Different views, held with conviction and systematically pursued, can have their place, but the education officer will want to be sure that this is not the result of mere default and that the end result is not simply chaos. Regular conferences of infant heads will give an opportunity to discuss not only the merits of the various methods but the way the approach to a reading scheme is organized. It is one aspect of the general question of the objectives to be reached by the end of the infant school course, which is a subject for discussion at conferences jointly with junior school heads. There can be organized opportunity for experiment with such innovations as the initial teaching alphabet, followed by sensitive administrative response to requests for resources to translate theory into practice. The freedom of the school and the teacher need not be imperilled by an organized approach: organizing can make sure that the freedom is put to good use.

Curriculum development

Freedom can begin to pall after a while and it can be very lonely: this may explain why although the curriculum is traditionally the responsibility of the individual head there is less variety than might be expected. Examinations such as the 'eleven plus' and the GCE have had a standardizing influence. But it is fair to say that the goals represented by examinations—though not necessarily the examinations themselves—have not been unwelcome to teachers.

Problems in practice

The CSE stemmed from the combined desires of parents, teachers and employers for an examination as a yardstick of measurement and an incentive, and the DES were reluctant to introduce it. As it happens the particular approach to this examination, shaped by teachers out of the actual work of the schools, acts as a spur to innovation rather than a curb.

Teachers have to re-think continually the main purposes of the curriculum and to work out their response to the challenge it presents. Nationally the Schools Council has sought to stimulate thinking and to indicate lines of attack on problems of research, investigation and experiment. All over the country development centres have sprung up. Their aims may be different: they may be concerned with primary education, or secondary, or with particular subjects. They may concentrate on organized activities or they may be places where teachers drop in casually to work out some problem or to meet like-minded people. At least one centre has an experimental full-time course for older children with the main object of working out new relationships between teacher and taught. The creation of many of them is the result of imaginative thinking and opportunist scheming by education officers.

After the 'eleven plus'

For the secondary schools the introduction of the CSE has given point to the study of curriculum development. The primary schools have the more difficult job of working out new objectives with the removal of the selection examination. For some heads the mere removal of a narrowing influence may be enough to stimulate new discovery and purpose. Certainly the whole trend of curriculum development is away from the limited approach imposed by this kind of examination. But others may find the vacuum unhealthy.

The end of the 'eleven plus' carries with it a need to consider the assumptions on which many schools have been run. Where does streaming fit in? Can a co-operative rather than a competitive spirit be encouraged? What new subjects can emerge? How can English and mathematics be developed on new lines? What testing is still needed and for what purpose? What goals can the junior school set for itself?

These are some of the issues. They cannot be settled by edict: individual inspiration ought to be shared. A new philosophy can only emerge from the hard work and self-analytical probings of the teachers themselves. It is the education officer's job to see that these efforts are co-ordinated and that the results have some chance of being implemented.

Courses for teachers

For many years local administrators have been sponsoring and taking part in week-end short courses for teachers. New patterns are now emerging both in form and content. Just as the idea of curriculum development stresses involvement by teachers so increasingly the pattern changes from lectures (followed by questions from the audience) to discussions, conferences, seminars and teach-ins in which the distinction between lecturer and audience disappears. New themes emerge : besides the traditional subjects of study, social questions, organizational problems and management techniques are beginning to come under the microscope. And weekend and holiday study is reinforced by in-service training for which teachers are given leave from duties to attend.

Longer courses are normally run by universities and colleges of education but the administrator's influence is likely to be felt in the kind of policy for secondment that he puts before his committee.

Part-time teachers in further education present a special problem and few authorities have yet developed satisfactory courses for those who, often without formal teaching qualifications, turn their hands to teaching adults. Although regional co-operation and links with university extra-mural departments and the Responsible Bodies are beginning to be effective in some areas, an organized attack is badly needed to improve the standard and standing of this neglected corner of the service.

Probationer teachers

Authorities have a special responsibility for the reception and initial on-the-job training of new teachers in their probationary year. Education officers organize each year a programme of interviews for potential teachers from colleges of education and pay special attention to the school in which the new teacher begins his or her service.

There is a social as well as a professional side to an authority's responsibility in the matter. Help in finding suitable lodgings, opportunities to meet other new teachers and the senior office staff, helpful booklets about the authority's policies and arrangements for payment of salaries, leave of absence and so on—all these can help to break the ice. Visits to the teacher in the classroom will be the responsibility of the adviser and many individual problems can be solved

Problems in practice

in the schools. But there are many things in which help is needed where it may be better to collect the new teachers together to allow them to exchange notes, to discuss questions of discipline, syllabuses, relations with senior colleagues, and a score of other questions the first year of teaching may bring.

Problems of judgement

Almost all administrative action needs judgement, so any selection of illustrative situations has to be arbitrary. Those briefly mentioned here try to cover some of the different kinds of judgement required.

Discretionary awards

The great issues of principle attract the headlines and perhaps bring most grey hairs. But month in month out, education authorities are deciding issues of peculiar difficulty : what they lack in drama they make up in impenetrability. The major decisions on university and comparable awards are national : it is a matter of interpreting regulations. But the incidental issues can be troublesome and there are many courses below graduate level and post-graduate which are at the discretion of the authority. The opposing criteria are concern for the student's well-being and concern for the ratepayers. The variables are the different standards of university and college recommendations and entrance standards. Another dilemma is whether the student's age or his academic qualifications should decide the level of his grant.

If from this mass of incompatible data reasonably coherent principles can be devised there will be still a need to watch out for changing circumstances such as new courses or parallels in other subjects. Precedent is important but it cannot be allowed to harden into an invariable rule.

Regional co-operation can help to avoid unnecessary anomalies through widely different practices in neighbouring areas. Occasional meetings of officers dealing with awards can help in other ways, too, for judgement in such finely shaded issues can be fortified if not improved by exchange of opinion and experience.

Courses in further education

The aim in decisions on awards is to reach a correct conclusion : In some problems the aim is somewhat different, to arrive at a satisfactory compromise. For example in fixing fees for further education courses there is a balance to be struck between fees that are too high for individual students—or those who sponsor them—and fees too low to provide a reasonable return for the outlay. In adult education classes the wish to make certain classes self-supporting may defeat its own object by limiting the number who enrol.

Allocation of resources

Another kind of judgement is a small scale version of the problem of priorities: in framing the estimates how much should be allowed to each branch of the service or to any particular project within a branch. The problem grows no less if the project involves subjects or equipment that the arbiter knows little about. In further education, for instance, even the principal of a technical college may know little about some of the subjects being taught in it. How then can he evaluate the needs of one department against another? And how can the education officer weigh up the claims of different colleges?

The technique may be based on his judgement of the reliability of the person making the claim; this will not take him all the way, but it is at the bottom of much decision-making of this kind. It will include if possible comparison with the costs of similar establishments or projects elsewhere. It may involve scrutiny by advisory committees (though they may be enthusiasts as much as scrutineers).

Nursery education

A refinement of the resources problem arises over nursery education: it is generally agreed that pre-school age education can be vital for some children but the statutory age-range has to be catered for first. There are severe limitations on authorities' freedom to provide nursery schools but even with permissive legislation the limitation on teaching staff would require nice decisions. Supposing a class is set up under a qualified teacher with a trained nursery assistant. What should happen if a teacher should suddenly leave the parent infant school and no replacement can be found? Should the teacher trained and appointed for nursery work transfer to the infant class leaving the nursery in the charge of the assistant; or should the infant classes grow to absurd proportions?

And what of pre-school playgroups? These voluntary groups perform a valuable function, in the absence of statutory provision. But since a small charge is made the service is mainly available to the better-off homes or those in which the mother wants to go out to work. Educational need would probably start elsewhere with the underprivileged home and the inadequate mother, with free provision. At present LEAs are not legally entitled to do more than advise these groups. The question is, should they try even if they were allowed? Apart from the issue of providing for those of statutory age first, there is a second problem. Ought help to start with those who help themselves or with those who need it most? Some would say that the demands of the articulate middle class are more likely to be heard and thus bring reform for all. Others fear that to allow spare accommodation to be used, even for a fee, may mean that when the time comes for advance every available corner will be already in use.

Problems with social and personal content

Individuals in the system

Many of the hardest decisions are those that impinge on personal and social life. In a providing service, like education, the administrator may feel happier on the relatively firm ground of creating institutions than in the more hazardous territory of concern for individuals. Any organization will, given half a chance, take over the people in it and one of the problems is how to prevent the creation of institutions and thereafter their smooth running from looming too large in the scheme of things.

Guidance and welfare services exist specifically for the individual but they can operate almost as if they were ends in themselves, self-evidently necessary, seeking material suitable for their own particular process and tending to reject problems of inconvenient shape and texture.

Whether society as a whole can yet formulate clear objectives for helping those who need guidance or special provision is doubtful. But within the bounds of the education service the administrator can determine intermediate objectives (the kind from which social as distinct from religious or moral progress generally comes). The concept of detecting, and putting right when possible, any factors—social, psychological, physical or academic—that prevent or hinder any child from taking full advantage of the educational facilities available is a starting point. The next stage is a re-examination of staffing resources and the way they are deployed, so that they can be regrouped as a complementary, cohesive unit, sensitive at the point of contact to the needs of those it serves.

The Plowden Report has questioned many administrative assumptions that point towards standardization. Can we not fix the time of admission to school, and of transfer to secondary education, according to individual readiness? Can we not look beneath the surface of poor attendance to the causes? How can we bring parents into the scheme of things attuning the service to the needs of the users? How can we discriminate in favour of those with the worst social handicaps? The transition the Report makes from critical analysis to practical solutions is a model for administrators.

Youth and community development

In the youth and community services it may be too cynical to say that present provision meets the needs of the providers better than those of those for whom it is intended. But there is something in it. Would not club leaders often be better employed as youth tutors in schools, colleges and factories? How serious are we about encouraging young people to handle their own affairs? Can some of the energy young people use in protest be channelled into positive action for those less fortunate than themselves? Is the assumed separation of interest between youth and adults really valid? What have we to offer for eighteen-year-olds who are already married?

To consider the young and the poor as different in kind from the rest of us is to continue nineteenth-century attitudes into a fluid society that rejects all patronage, protocol and mythology, however well-intentioned. Whether the rejection is achieved peacefully or through violence will depend largely on how far the social institutions can wean themselves away from assumptions. That youth and community services should seem a far cry from the unrest and upheaval of student power and football crowd vandalism is a measure of their inadequacies. The 1944 Act talks of the provision of recreation and social and physical training. To identify the community's needs and involve the community in providing them; to identify common benefits and establish communal responsibility for them— these aims come nearer the problems of our time, when the welfare state has removed many of the inhibitions of fear and at the same time obscured the demarcation lines of responsibility.

Postscript

Organization; the quality of education; judgement; social and personal problems. This formidable list indicates something of the range of types of problem for the education officer. If he sometimes frets at the occasional assumption within local government that educational administration is no different from other branches and asks for special treatment it may perhaps be special pleading. On the other hand this attitude is not without factual basis. This chapter and the two that preceded it are full of reminders of the tensions—between democracy and efficiency, planning and pragmatism, philosophy and procedures—discussed in Chapter One.

Yet when we turn to look at the tools of the education officer's trade, the methods he uses to solve his problems, we cannot assume revolutionary changes. The methods will be considered within the context of the existing system; as ways in which the resources and practices already available might be used to better advantage.

9

Committee work

Decision-making on important issues in education is inextricably bound up with committee work. Some would say that 'inextricably' is exactly the right word, that we encumber ourselves with meetings. There is a myth that committees are always vague and hesitant and an implication that individuals are always swift and incisive when it comes to making decisions. This bears no relation to the facts.

In the first place only the existence of a committee to which they must work seems to stir some administrators into activity. And all committees are not alike. Perhaps there are too many of them; perhaps they are prone to seek compromise solutions, but both these features really reflect the importance we attach to democracy. Committees are no worse than the people who are on them and in local government the council and the great majority of members of its policy-making committees are chosen by the electorate.

In particular the biggest single factor in the success or otherwise of a committee is the calibre of its chairman. The Chairman of the Education Committee is thus a very important person in the professional life of the Chief Education Officer and the chairmen of the sub-committees are likely to be equally prominent in the lives of the senior officers responsible for the different branches of the service.

Education officers themselves have to act as chairmen of all manner of committees, from internal policy discussions to regional and even national advisory bodies. Yet characteristically they act as secretary and professional adviser to policy-making elected committees and this chapter will deal mainly with that aspect of the education officer's work. A representative of the Clerk of the Council may well perform some secretarial function for the education committee and its sub-committees, such as keeping the minutes and formally introducing each item, but the education officer almost always has the major responsibility of compiling agendas and advising the committee on policy. For convenience it is assumed here that he performs all the functions of a secretary together with his advisory role.

The chairman

A good chairman can get something out of an unwieldy, badly briefed, procedureless and badly documented committee, but ideal size, organization and precision count for nothing with an incompetent leader. A chairman's role varies according to the nature of the committee—its scope, purpose, regularity of function and degree of permanence—and to the nature of his own appointment— whether he is elected by the members or appointed from outside; whether he is for one meeting or a series; whether he is likely to remain in spite of changes in political control, and so on. Perhaps even more than this it depends on his own personality, the view he himself takes of his role and his skill in carrying it out. The power of a determined, ambitious and skilful chairman is very considerable indeed.

His function in the single meeting shows that the chairman's basic role includes all the power needed to cover almost any extension of it. He is there to keep order and to see that the business is got through. This means that he is the focal point for everyone, the person to whom each member of the committee must address his remarks, so that everybody is not talking at once or alternatively one person is not hogging the whole show.

Some chairmen may be content with discharging the basic function : others can go well beyond it. For, of course, the chairman can in practice speak himself whenever he likes in a debate; he can initiate discussion or close it, and decide what is relevant and therefore admissible; his own remarks are always in order (though he may agree to withdraw them or wish he had not said them on occasion). Beyond this from time to time in a meeting he may have to—or wish to—represent the members of the committee in a disagreement with the secretary : alternatively he may sometimes represent the secretary against the members : or one half of the membership against the other. He controls these realignments and can use this factor to advantage. On procedural matters (which may well have influence well beyond their apparent scope) he is also the arbiter in disputes of this kind. He often may decide when the debate must end and when, or whether, a vote is to be taken.

Another aspect of his role may give him power in an unexpected way. He can ask questions at any time he likes and unlike other members can insist upon an answer as a condition of proceeding with the business. This is of greater value where there is continuity of chairmanship rather than a single performance : for of course it can lead to briefing in advance by the secretary and this gives the chairman his greatest strength of all—greater knowledge than other members.

After the meeting the chairman's influence may still continue. He may be sent the draft minutes for approval. Some would argue that it is the secretary's inalienable right to be regarded as the sole judge of fact of what took place; but without the chairman's support the minutes could, conceivably, be overthrown as a record, so prudence suggests that wherever possible the chairman is consulted.

Quite often the chairman has delegated powers to act on behalf of his committee between meetings and although it may be under-stood that these are emergency powers and his actions usually have to be reported to the committee for confirmation, nevertheless here is a great extension of authority. Like the question of the minutes it is bound up with the secretary's power : an alternative to delega-tion of interim powers to the chairman is delegation to the secretary. This may to some committees be a simple matter of convenience, but often it goes deeper. Where the secretary is a permanent official and the chairman is elected, the committee's delegation will reflect their whole attitude towards officials : if they fear bureaucracy above all else they will prefer the chairman to have charge.

Yet they may not be too happy about that, either, if party politics is involved. And for some committees, added to the fear of the chairman pulling some devilish political trick, is anxiety lest he fall into the clutches of the bureaucrats. Most elected chairmen, given authority to act between meetings, are shy of using it without advice from the officials. Frequently the initiative will come from the official who may well be the first to know of the problem. So the opposition party, especially if they mistrust officials, may seek to curb the power of the chairman.

The straight alternative, dealing with everything in committee, is never wholly satisfactory. First, it may mean frequent meetings and vast agendas, full of trivia. Second, it emphasizes the weakness of the committee system, its intermittent life, and consequent periodic death. Experiments such as delegating authority to a small executive group (including opposition party members) may make getting a quick decision virtually impossible. So in the end it usually happens that the chairman has the delegated power and takes advice from the secretary.

Most committees have in fact a built-in assumption that the chairman's role will continue outside the walls of the committee room. In national committees for instance, where a report is prepared for presentation to the government, it is usual for the report to be given the name of the chairman—such as the Robbins or Plowden Report—and for the chairman to be regarded as the spokesman for the report in the subsequent discussions, including any arguments with the government. In local government, chairmanship of a standing committee is an office in which presiding over meetings may be only a small part. In the first place many important decisions will in fact be made by the majority party before the actual committee meeting: the chairman's role in the party group meeting may be to argue a case, to advise, or just to take instructions. Then again the chairman will be answerable for his committee's decisions in the City or County Council meeting at which controversial decisions by the component committees are debated, usually on political rather than specialist lines. To the public the chairman represents the policy and the department carrying it out and he will be invited to many functions, ceremonial, social and investigatory. He may discover, sometimes after he has accepted a job, that presiding over meetings of the committee is just the tip of the iceberg.

But we must look at him first in the committee setting. The chairman's job in the committee meeting, apart from the formalities and the general order-keeping function, is to present each item on the agenda to the committee, to ensure that it is properly discussed and to bring it to a specific conclusion. His task is not to anticipate or forestall the discussions, even under the guise of saving time.

The best chairmen seem to:

a Get together all the information possible about the meeting beforehand: ask for a brief from the secretary and read it;
b Consult the secretary in advance about last-minute information and possible problems;

c Introduce the subject and pick out the essentials of the problem;
alternatively ask the secretary to do so;

d Encourage discussion, short of pointing the finger at individuals
and obliging them to contribute whether they have anything to
say or not;

e Encourage brevity (by example as well as precept) particularly
on early items so that there is no rush later when members are
tired, tempers may be frayed and time is short;

f Try to reach a decision, though preferably not by a vote.

Voting ought to be reserved for the most final of showdowns
where a decision is vital and the committee sharply divided. It is
a divisive influence and it can have unfortunate repercussions: to
argue and lose is one thing, but to have your defeat publicly labelled
and recorded is another. It can lead to aggressive counter-attacks on
later items, including voting against someone because he voted
against you before; or it can lead to sulky and brooding reaction
or loss of confidence. This is not to say that 'the feeling of the
meeting' is enough: this can mean that the chairman and the
secretary carve it up between them afterwards, and although most
members of committee are cheerfully content to have this happen
to some extent, there are limits. The wise chairman will summarize
what he takes to be findings of the meeting and ask whether the
committee agree.

The secretary

Discussion of the chairman's role has inevitably involved frequent
reference to that of the secretary. The two jobs have much in
common. Ideally they are complementary: if so, cynics on the
committee may well consider them partners in crime. Inevitably
their paths cross and recross, and it is a happy chance if they like
each other.

One thing they have in common is that their basic role gives
them more potential power than might appear on the surface. Even
a committee clerk—the secretary in his humblest form—has knowledge of the correct procedure, information about the powers and
terms of reference of the committee, and possibly continuity of office
to strengthen his influence. If he has to write the minutes then his
importance is increased, and if he prepares the agenda item he adds
a new dimension to his role. The administrator as secretary will
normally perform these duties—or have them performed for him—
and will often add the job of adviser on policy or technical matters

as well. If, as in local government, he is permanent while his chairman and many of the members change from time to time, he is likely to have a great deal of responsibility, perhaps even (the naked word) power.

One of the least publicized but most telling factors in an administrative relationship is who was there first. The one who knows the ropes has more than a head start. So a secretary—particularly a permanent one—already *in situ* may have quite an advantage over a new chairman—particularly one whose tenure is less secure. It will be part of the secretary's duties to help the chairman with his new job, and the guidance may be so great as to make the chairman heavily dependent. This situation may seem ideal to some, but the good administrator will not wish to enjoy the satisfaction of this sort of relationship too long. He will take pride in helping to make the chairman strong and independent, knowing by so doing he is helping to foster democracy and good government, which is what, above all else, he is paid to do. In practice, however, the administrator's sights are probably set on nearer, less elevated, targets. He will be concerned with the conduct of the meeting and the success of his own proposals.

On both these scores a close relationship with the chairman is important, and however knowledgeable or dominant the chairman may be the secretary has certain advantages. He can always get his blow in first; and he is likely to know more about the situation than anyone else. For instance the purpose of a preliminary briefing session is to give the chairman information. But it can also be an opportunity for the secretary to find out what is in the chairman's mind. Forewarned, he will be able to pay special attention to certain points that he then knows are certain to be raised : nothing increases his prestige more than to be able to give a good answer to a difficult question; and this is more likely to happen if he knows the question in advance. Again, in an advisory committee whose function is to produce a report, a strong chairman may impose his view on the committee and this may be evident in the report. But the drafting of the report normally falls to the secretary and this may consciously or unconsciously alter the balance of views.

Some would say that the secretary should claim sole responsibility for the content of agendas, but whatever the theory, it is sometimes wise for a secretary to consult the chairman. Nevertheless the initiative normally lies with the secretary and if the chairman disagrees with the content of the agenda the onus is on him to put it right. Perhaps the secretary is on slightly stronger grounds if he wishes to claim the undisputed right to produce a true record of the proceedings : prudence still suggests consultation.

Any suggestion of a possible power struggle between secretary and chairman is normally very wide of the mark. It is not a promising approach for either. Perhaps outside the meeting struggle may be possible or even from the administrator's point of view desirable. During the meeting the two must, and almost invariably do, work together. Indeed for many committees the chief danger is that they will work so closely together as to appear to carve anything up between them, leaving nothing of any importance for the committee to decide.

Still there has to be partnership. Someone has to see the rules are observed; someone has to introduce the subject; someone has to outline the relevant facts; someone has to bring the discussion to a close; and someone has to record what was decided. The secretary's job is to see that the chairman does whichever of these he wants to do, to help him if necessary and to do the rest himself.

The education officer will not usually be in the position of simply expressing a point of view in the committee : indeed sometimes he will try to avoid 'taking sides'. He will explain, he will advocate, giving his reasons, and frequently his ideas will be unchallenged : they may be the only ones expressed. The points at issue will range from the microscopic to the fundamental. Whatever the problem and whatever his views the good administrator probably always has in the back of his mind the aim of winning the whole war not just individual skirmishes.

The war, however, is not a private battle. It is the struggle to see that the basic purposes of the service are constantly kept before the committee. The characteristic, and most fruitful, role of the administrator is to make sure the committee are constantly aware of the implications of the proposals they make. Sometimes he may sound, and feel, like the skeleton at the feast. This is where a sense of humour will help him, and his committee.

Types of committee

The young administrator is unlikely to find himself acting as secretary to the full education committee : that is normally the function of the Chief Education Officer. 'Taking the committee' as the professionals call it is likely to mean something humbler for the beginner : it is a mark of distinction when he is allowed to take a sub-committee of the main committee. Although relationships between secretary and chairman, officer and members are basically similar, there are differences of approach related to the nature of the committee.

Thus the education committee itself is a deliberative assembly, usually meeting in public. Members approve the proceedings of sub-committees and take the opportunity to air their views on controversial issues. There is in the nature of things little policy-building or patient exploration of possibilities. Consequently the Chief Education Officer may say very little and may confine his contributions to matters of fact and guidance about the implications of what is being proposed.

In contrast it is unfortunately true that sometimes at a meeting of the managers of a primary school most of the proceedings may seem to consist of reports by the head or the education officer. Between these extremes the administrator will find himself cast in a great variety of roles and he is likely to have to learn how to pitch his contributions at the right level through practical experience. He may begin with an advisory committee.

The term advisory committee can be applied to so many groups that it is hard to be specific about what it means. There is an element of advisory work in almost all committees : very few bodies simply utter pronouncements without giving reasons or supporting comments. In this sense governing bodies, whether they pass resolutions or not, essentially act in an advisory capacity to the education committee. Even amongst advisory committees proper, there is an almost infinite range, from nationally sponsored standing committees, to small local groups set up for specific purposes and disbanded immediately afterwards. Whatever the level the attitude of members to their job is likely to be ambivalent. On the one hand there is nothing so pleasant as to give advice without any of the tiresome trouble of having to put into practice. On the other hand, people whose advice is sought tend to feel that it should be taken.

In this context serving on an advisory committee may be a suitable means of employment only for those of placid temperament or, conversely, of iron will and resolution. For in addition to the normal hazards of trying to get a committee to accept one's point of view there is the uncertainty about whether the collective advice will be taken or not afterwards. Administrators serving or advising advisory committees (the third remove from reality) would undoubtedly welcome some formula that could ensure success. Regrettably there appears to be no such panacea, which may explain why inexperienced or subordinate staff are often despatched to perform the miracle.

They, poor souls, are frequently caught in withering cross-fire. Superior committees may be displeased that the advisory committee have been allowed (even, they may hint, encouraged) to put up such unacceptable advice. And, when the advisory committee next meet, they may be even angrier that their advice has not been taken, and, in extreme cases, may not be above suggesting that it is because their case has been badly presented.

An administrator who has done his best, fought hard and lost, may find this the unkindest cut of all. There are, perhaps, palliatives. First, he should if possible make quite sure he knows in advance what kind of advice is likely to be unacceptable to the superior committee, and he should run the risk of being thought a sombre fellow by the advisory committee by conveying his misgivings at every stage. If the committee, as they may well do, decide to disregard this interference, then they must be prepared for possible setbacks later. The administrator may not be more popular for having been right, but it is conceivable that his advice will be more regarded next time; even if it is not he will have a clear conscience which is not to be despised as a solace amidst unpleasant circumstances.

But, second, he should try to get the committee to present their findings in the right way. Eloquence and enthusiasm are not enough : they will achieve nothing if the fundamental issues are vaguely stated or are assumed to be self-evident. If the committee anticipate possible difficulties they will be able to pay special attention to their arguments at the relevant points. If expense is a likely difficulty, for instance, they can try to show where possible savings might be made. They can try to secure agreement in principle for their recommendations, for implementation when circumstances allow. They should try to see that their case includes strong arguments, not just conclusions.

Many of these points apply to working with sub-committees of the education committee. They are not advisory, but policy-making committees, but they may still have trouble in securing acceptance of the policies they recommend to the parent body. In relation to an advisory body a superior committee can conceivably, if not very tactfully, reject advice and turn to other sources for it. An education committee cannot do this to one of its own sub-committees, but it can refer back an unacceptable recommendation for further consideration.

It is in the sub-committees where the real significance of arguments about the proper relationship between members and the

officers is felt. This is because it is at this level that policy is effectively made, so that the officer has his best chance to impress or
offend his employers by the way he conducts himself and by the
quality of the advice he gives. It is here, too, that the basic question
is settled of how much should be delegated to officers and how much
left to committee decision.

Discussion of this issue often arouses strong emotions. It is almost
always hypothetical and so of little value. One of the best books
on committees and their workings is *Government by Committee* by
K. C. Wheare. It is a wise, witty and valuable contribution to
learning on a difficult subject. The author gives the opinion that
'it is the job of the committee, within the limits of the powers conferred upon it by the council, and by Parliament, to decide what
shall be done, to appoint those who are to do it, and to see that they
do it well'. This is probably as good a definition as it is possible
to get and the subsequent discussion of the practical implications
and reservations is excellent. Yet it is possible to agree with every
word, but still to find that in practice there would be disagreement
on the interpretation, and furthermore disagreement so profound as
to amount almost to rejection of the proposition.

For what does 'to decide what shall be done' mean? It is only
by examining specific issues that any meaningful discussion can
take place. Does it mean, with the Maud Committee, that committees should be 'deliberative, not executive', that elected members
should concern themselves only with policy? Who decides what is
policy and what an application of it? In practice there is a serious
objection to the views of the Maud Report in that thinking about
general principles does not come easily to any human being and
it is certainly not a conspicuous feature of the normal approach of
most local councillors. Decisions on policy have to be based on
knowledge, and this can only be built up from concrete examples of
the problem that has to be solved. Thereafter it may perhaps be
possible to establish general principles, but there is little profit in
trying to begin from abstractions, nor are committees likely to
embrace the principle of 'policy only' throughout their service from
the outset. At best it can only be a trend, a movement towards
greater delegation, relying fundamentally on mutual trust between
members and officers.

Elected members, like most people, find the particular examples
easier to handle than the attempt to draw up a general scheme.
Further they may well acquire a taste for making these decisions,
particularly if they have a bearing on something, or someone,

familiar to them. Thus they may cling to 'treating each case on its merits', a much over-worked approach.

Theoretical discussion about the extent to which members should delegate to officers is of little value. What is needed is patient and systematic examination, by committee members and officers together, of the actual problems that arise and the kind of solutions that suit the particular circumstances.

Outside committees the relationships between members and officers are almost invariably good, and very fruitful. They are often conscious of working together for the common good, through some problem that arises, in a way that is rarely possible in a committee. Members are able to take up complaints or enquiries from constituents, to serve on advisory bodies, to visit institutions and to perform other civic duties with very great effect. Yet their most important function, establishing policy for the various services, is sometimes subject to almost unbelievable, self-imposed restrictions, both in procedural obscurities and in excessive attention to the question of proper relationships with officials.

An approach that may fall some way short of being a panacea, but that nevertheless can transform the effectiveness, morale and mutual confidence of members and officials is the working party. This is, of course, still a committee, but with a difference. The rules of procedure can be much less formal and, most important of all, officers and councillors can serve together as members. At its best—which means amongst other things when the group is small—the working party can get to the root of a matter much quicker than any formal committee. There is, after all, a world of difference in the meaning of the phrases 'sitting in committee' and 'sitting round a table' although the physical posture and the personnel may be the same. Nor is this a mere Machiavellian attempt to secure greater influence for officials by installing them as members as well as secretaries: for the officer, too, gives up a good deal of his traditional authority. The working party can be what a more formal committee may find it difficult to become, men and women working together without any artificial barriers towards a common end and for the common good.

We shall return to this notion later, for it has a bearing on the all-important question of relationships. The purpose here has been to consider committees as the source of authority, and therefore decision-making, for the education officer. In the next chapter we consider the basis of information without which decision-making is an empty phrase.

10

Information

Decision-making needs a basis of information: it cannot operate in a vacuum. It is true that some administrators put up remarkable virtuoso performances, at times appearing to manage without any information at all; and others seem to dislike being hindered by the facts. But these are Parkinsonian characters from whom we must avert our eyes. Many experienced administrators would equate information with knowledge of their service, and clearly this must play an important part, particularly in education. For management purposes, however, the most significant aspect of information is its processing and use as a basis for policy decisions and future planning. Can it be so ordered as to present a clear picture of what has happened in the past, what the situation is at present and what ought to happen in the future?

There must always be some attempt at selection and ordering of facts whether the administrator is presenting a case for decision to someone else or trying to make up his own mind. Can the present-day education officer rely solely on his brains and his experience? The ordinary processes of reasoning (perhaps, on reflection, not quite so ordinary) are the best single method in any of these transactions, but the question is whether unaided this is enough. Reason is not quite the pure instrument of absolute truth it once seemed to be, and experience, though in some ways a help, can lead to assumptions that the future will always follow the pattern of the past.

There is of course a very real danger that in dealing with questions that are so complicated and profound as to be frightening, people who can produce an apparatus of scientific expertise, may draw attention away from the matter to be decided by dwelling on the means of making the decision. One fear is that the experts will hold sway by blinding us with science. Another is that those who have to make the decisions may use their findings to support existing prejudices. If the expert is preoccupied with method, with admiring his own skill, he may, like the atomic scientists, find that he has created a monster. The administrator, then, is likely to be of more service as an evaluator than as a potential expert himself. He should know enough about the methods and findings of scientific analysis to use them and to see the limitations of their use.

In the public service the limitations may be greater than in industry because of the nature of the problems that have to be solved. Objectives are easier to formulate and success is easier to measure in an enterprise where production and profit are the aims. Decision-making and planning may be harder still in the education service with its built-in democratic safeguards. Some of the problems we have been discussing demand a degree of understanding and sensitivity not normally associated with computers or their advocates.

It would be comforting to think that the hostility of some practising administrators towards the new sciences and techniques of management—computers, operational research, statistics and other aids to decision-making—was based on reasoning of this kind. Certainly it is hard to argue with those who suggest (*a*) that decision-making is more subjective and more sophisticated than the scientific approach would have us believe, and (*b*) that the aids, the machinery, the procedures, the formulae can be little more than an elaborate smoke-screen, a refuge from harsh reality. But this is a far cry from discrediting the whole apparatus: the organized collection and presentation of information is an important aid to decision-making even if it is not to be confused with the decision-making itself.

The procedures and patterns used in the public services may be a strong disincentive to try anything new and they may impose a strait-jacket where freedom would achieve more. But there is often greater freedom than at first sight appears.

Financial control is a good example. The traditional attitude in a spending department is to regard the Treasury as an enemy to be outwitted: the aim is to get as much as they can in the estimates and then spend as much as they can, inside or outside the estimates. It has taken a series of economic crises to bring about the beginnings of a new attitude in which it is accepted that there is never likely to be enough money to satisfy the ideal and that an essential part of administration is getting the best out of the available resources. Of all the elements in the conflict about who should manage the nation's affairs this is the most crucial : if traditional-style administrators cannot do the job they must expect to be replaced by those who can. The problem is not just one of making ends meet, but one requiring forethought about the information needed, skill in getting it, and proper use of the results as a basis for decision and control.

The conventional instrument for manipulating money is the budget and it may be useful to see how far this can be made to help in planning and disposition of the use of resources. Because more radical methods such as programme-planning-budgeting systems are as yet rare the traditional pattern is assumed.

Budgeting

A local budget has an assortment of aims. It (i) fixes the rate of local taxation, (ii) analyses expenditure and income for the committees, (iii) forms a plan of action (since inclusion in the approved estimates is usually, though not always, taken to give approval to take action for the purpose for which it was intended) and (iv) is a check on whether money is spent on the purpose for which it was approved. None of them need prevent its use as an instrument of administrative control.

'The budget' or 'the estimates' usually means the annual revenue budget : that is, transactions affecting the deficiency of the rate fund. They exclude for the most part the acquisition or disposal of fixed assets, which are dealt with in the capital budget, but they include debt charges incurred in borrowing to finance capital projects. It is rare for local authorities to plan revenue expenditure more than one year ahead, although forecasts extending over longer periods are required by the government for calculation of grants.

Long-term capital programmes are prepared listing proposed future capital projects, most of which will be financed from loans : the annual capital budget crystallizes the expected capital transactions for the immediate period ahead. Each of the two budgets has to be considered in relation to the other. For example, a proposed new school has its repercussions for the revenue estimates—extra staff, extra materials and, of course, debt charges and rates.

The revenue estimates are likely to be presented to the Council in January for approval or possible revision so that they can come into force the following 1st April, the start of the financial year. Preparation of the education estimates has to begin in the summer so that governors and managers of schools and divisional executives can see them in the early autumn before they go to the sub-committees and the education committee. Thus the span of the proposals will cover over eighteen months from inception to the end of the financial year. This is a pity, but the biggest complication is that the academic year extends from September to August, which means that in budgeting, for instance, for new staff starting work in September the estimates have to include seven-twelfths of the full annual cost. The adjustment that has to be made later when the staff are there for a full year is a great source of confusion. Worse than this it makes comparison of estimates from year to year difficult and so diminishes one of the possible uses of the estimates as a source of planning.

Whenever possible policy decisions need to be made before the estimates are produced. The estimates themselves are not usually used as a policy-making instrument but rather a means of giving effect to policy: it would be too big a job to consider all policy issues at the same time as the finances of the enterprise. Yet decisions made about what is put in the estimates can restrict the possibilities of future action, so the policy should be settled first. The estimates are also part of a stock-taking exercise, a way of examining the implications of existing policy. They can hardly be over-emphasized as a management tool, therefore.

An education committee's expenditure is usually so big that the estimate is divided up by sub-committees. Within each sub-committee's sector expenditure and income are set out under a large number of sub-headings, the lines of the estimate, according to a standard formula agreed nationally by local authority treasurers.

The figures in the sample page shown overleaf are imaginary but possible.

The number of different figures given for each line of the estimates varies, but is usually something like this:

1	2	3	4	5
Previous year's actual expenditure	Item concerned	Current year's original estimate	Current year's revised estimate	Next year's proposed estimate

Primary Schools

Expenditure		Income	
Employees	£	**Sales**	£
Salaries and Wages—		Sale of materials	1,700
Teaching Staff	3,135,649		
Caretakers and Cleaners	364,767	**Fees and Charges**	
Administrative Staff	65,041	Tuition Fees	140
Nursery & Welfare Assistants	77,571	Parental Contributions—	
National Insurance	140,137	Clothing	30
Superannuation Charges—		Contributions by other	
Teachers (Superannuation)		Local Authorities	101,925
Acts	251,005		
Local Gov't Superannuation		**Rents**	4,500
Acts	7,805		
		Miscellaneous Income	5
Running Expenses			
Premises—			
Repairs	150,000		
Painting	39,100		
Alterations	5,000		
Upkeep of Grounds	83,403		
Fuel, Light, Water and			
Cleaning Materials	221,400		
Furniture and Fittings	21,000		
Rent and Rates	150,275		
Supplies and Services—			
Books	} 187,344		
Stationery and Materials			
Educational Equipment	7,000		
Cleaning, Domestic and			
Administrative Equipment	10,000		
Clothing and Uniforms	2,700		
Laundry	4,200		
Hired & Contracted Services	—		
Transport	60		
Establishment Expenses—			
Printing, Stationery, Postages			
and Sundries	5,300		
Travelling & Subsistence of Staff	1,000		
Telephones	7,400		
Debt Management Expenses	3,266		
Other Establishment Expenses	2,595		
Agency Services—			
Rendered by other Local			
Authorities	61,669		
Rendered by other			
Council Committees	3,000		
Miscellaneous Expenses—			
Educational Visits	7,800		
Aids to Pupils—			
Clothing and Footwear	2,600		
Fees and Expenses	2,850		
Travel—Home to School	2,200		
Travel—Other	13,100		
Other Expenses	2,283		
Debt Charges			
Interest	116,350		
Redemption	109,541		
Land Transfer Annuities—			
Payable	406		
Land Transfer Annuities—			
Receivable	Cr. 167		
	5,264,650		108,300

The object is to show up variations from year to year. The revised estimate for the current year can be just as revealing as any of the others.

The amount of detail in the printed estimates put before the council will depend on the members' wishes and on the treasurer's influence. There are arguments for and against a lot of detail.

On the one hand members need detailed information if they are to judge whether or not the estimate is reasonable. Over-provision shows up better in a detailed analysis. Furthermore once a detailed estimate is approved financial control within the department can be much easier if individuals are given responsibility for specific lines or parts of lines.

On the other hand the detail of estimates running into many millions of pounds can be confusing to members. Too much detail can also lead to over-estimating through leaving safety margins on many heads instead of a few. And if there is no virement (freedom to use up savings on one line to meet deficiencies on others) the framework can be too rigid so that the committee may later need constantly to be asked to make adjustments.

A reasonable compromise is to have the simplest possible estimate but with full supporting information about its make-up for any members who want to probe more deeply and for administrative use afterwards. The supporting information may be, for instance, analysis of the make-up of each line, or groupings and comparisons of various lines with previous years. A line-by-line analysis might include :

1 a breakdown of the current year's original estimate;
2 the amount of, and reasons for, variation between that and the current year's revised estimate of probable expenditure;
3 the amount of and reasons for variations between the current year's original estimate and the next year's (or as an alternative between the current year's probable expenditure and next year's estimate).

The breakdown might include such things as the actual number of staff employed and expected to be employed, the number of pupils and students used as the basis for capitation allowances and the dates by which new establishments are expected to open.

Another kind of analysis tries to isolate reasons for increased expenditure by identifying, say, inescapable commitments (from say national salary awards or debt charges); maintenance of premises; expenditure needed to implement policy decisions already taken;

and the cost of proposed new ventures. It may be helpful to compare the estimates of the different sub-committees to see what percentage increase on the previous year is proposed for each. There may be tables and charts showing the level of price increases for various commodities, the numbers of pupils, students and staff, the *per capita* costs of various branches of the service and so on. The immediate object of the exercise is to justify the money being spent, but it has a long-term value in picking out trends and tendencies that may show up strengths and weaknesses in the organization. One of the sins that beset public administration is 'habitual spending'. Freed from the necessity of making a profit each year, it is too easy to assume that everything that was spent last year will need to be spent again : the better the breakdown the more light will be cast on these dusty corners and the more money will be available for other purposes.

Capital forecasts vary according to local preference. A common pattern is to divide the forecast into programme years and to sub-divide each year between (*a*) schemes in progress (*b*) those about to start (*c*) those approved by central government and local council (*d*) those submitted for government approval but not yet decided and (*e*) those awaiting local council approval. The estimated costs for each year will show loan charges and running costs, sub-divided into (*a*) land acquisition, (*b*) building and (*c*) other costs including equipment.

Annual capital estimates, like longer-term forecasts, are likely to be much less accurate than revenue estimates. Discrepancies between projects submitted to central government and those actually approved are a normal hazard; the pace of planning and building fluctuates considerably; and costs change between the stages of proposals and completion. All kinds of devices are used to try to keep to the forecast level of expenditure—switches from one programme year to another (on paper, that is) and last-minute inclusions or exclusions. But there is inevitably a lack of precision and the revenue estimates are much more use as a management tool.

From the original drafts the revenue estimates are subjected to a long process of scrutiny and pruning, first by officers, then by sub-committees, then by spending committees, and then usually by a finance committee who in practice fix the level of expenditure, usually less than the spending committees have asked for. So the process of pruning has to begin all over again.

Perhaps the finance committee may itself decide what items should be cut from the spending committee's budget. This is unusual and obviously fraught with hazards. Apart from the possibility of errors it is usually thought only decent to allow the spending committee to decide where the cuts must come. At this stage the careful analysis made in preparing the estimates pays dividends, for it is much easier to make reductions in the right places if the relative disposition of the various increases originally proposed is known.

Opinions may vary about the ethics of including sums in the estimates for the specific purpose of removal when cuts are called for. Cushioning prevents the knife doing too much damage, and outrageously brutal reductions by finance committees may provoke precautionary measures in subsequent years. But an inflated estimate earns the estimator a bad reputation and this may strengthen the conviction by the finance committee that cuts can take place with safety. Perhaps the administrator should think of himself as a shopkeeper: if he is after a quick profit he may pitch his prices high; but if he wants to stay in business he will be more moderate.

It will almost certainly fall to the chief officer to make suggestions about where the cuts should fall with least harm to the service. He will have in mind what he believes to be the main projects the committee would wish to preserve, but much will depend on technical knowledge of the estimates to know where small, painless incisions can be made. The treasurer will need to be consulted: partly because he can help to identify relatively plush areas and partly because he will wish to ensure that there are not too many 'paper' cuts—mere reductions of figures on lines where the money will have to be spent regardless of what the estimates say, for instance to pay the salaries of people already in the service.

And very often the officer's suggestions will be the ones to be adopted. When they are presented many people may disagree: each will wish to have something or other reinstated. But the claims tend to cancel each other out and it is rare that anyone is able to say what should go out to make room for their particular project: it is easier to suggest things to be left in than those to be cut out.

Considering how crucial the exercise is it can hardly be said to be well done in most education offices. The procedures tend to be traditional and the attitude to them somewhat negative. It is a chore and it is often scrambled through. Part of the difficulty is that the education estimates are extremely complicated and require a good deal of finesse to manipulate. But the men with the most finesse and knowledge are in the treasurer's department and, although they can and do help in preparation of estimates, there is a certain ambiguity in their role that can lead to tension and perhaps mistrust. There is much to be said for the employment of an accountant within the education office. In an office of any size he can save more than his salary throughout the year by his advice and expertise. And at estimates time he can transform a pedestrian and casual affair into a precisely articulated exercise that is central to the department's thinking. As it is the tradition tends to be passed on informally with inadequate documentation and little or no training for those responsible for it. For this reason if for no other it is reasonable to claim that bad estimating is usually the result of incompetence rather than guile.

Tabulated information

The estimates can be a mere description of what goes on or an adjunct of policy making. The same is true of much other information collected in public affairs, notably of course, statistics. There are all over the country well-meaning fellows gathering information year by year, making it up into tables and charts, and neither they nor anyone else are quite sure of what it is for.

The name and the use of statistics has a curious, ambivalent, half-baked status in administration. Most of us use statistics or think we do : we 'get them out'; we may want to know the average cost of this or the increased cost of that over last year. Yet there is deep suspicion of the rigorous disciplines and abstruse formulae of the statistician. There are no prizes for guessing why : very few people understand them.

To most education officers the word is probably associated with annual returns and other routine presentations usually designed to describe what has already happened. Statistics does mean numerical data that describe or illustrate; but it also means the science of analysing the data. Any old set of figures is not statistics—although popular usage says it is. The figures have to demonstrate something. They usually do this by comparison and from the techniques of comparing the actual with the past has been developed that of predicting the probable.

It would be of no service either to education officers or to statistics to attempt a do-it-yourself guide in a few paragraphs. The extent to which statistical methods can be used will depend on available resources as well as on the interest and attitude of the administrator. But it is not unreasonable to suggest as a first stage regular review of the existing processes of information collection and distribution.

Education departments like other public services tend to produce facts and figures in great profusion. Their production is as often as not the result of tradition: they are collected in the same form each time, published with a sigh of relief and forgotten until the next occasion. Members of the staff asked to produce them may not be told their precise purpose; indeed that may not be known beyond the fact that a committee requires them. For their part the committee, inheriting a legacy from distant predecessors, may be equally in the grip of tradition.

People rarely question the format of statistical information but they do frequently ask for more. Different sub-committees may be interested in different aspects of the same problem. One result is that the same people may be asked for similar or identical information two or three times. In a good information system the amount and kind required are reviewed regularly and collection and presentation are considered together in advance.

Quantification often extends beyond figures into the realm of surveys. The form in which the questions are asked may imperil the process here from the outset by allowing too much latitude in reply or requiring clairvoyance from the respondent. If opinion is involved there are extra hazards: for usable answers it is necessary to ask the right questions. Public opinion polls have, whatever else they have done, shown up some of the dangers of sloppy or slanted questioning. It is no use asking for instance 'Do you approve of war?' and expecting a significant yes or no answer. The qualifications and reservations most people would associate with such a question have to be put into the questions or else they will appear in, and make a nonsense of, the answers.

Confusions and distortions which are only partly inherent, and which may be largely the result of inadequate techniques, lead some to under-rate the value of quantifying and codifying information and to place too narrow a limit on the range of a statistical approach. Some things are not susceptible to statistical analysis. Other matters require such an elaborate framework and such sophisticated interpretation that a statistical approach is not worthwhile. But sometimes the trouble is simply lack of forethought and inadequate presentation. And that can be avoided.

Operational research

It would be cynical to divide education officers into two categories in their attitude to operational research—those who curl up their lips at the very mention and those who have acquired, in self-defence, a few vogue words to throw back at the O and M team. Yet the ranks of those who use it are not very numerous.

True, it cannot be claimed that the activities of the Local Government Operational Research Unit have yet—in such matters as school population forecasting or computerized school timetables—shown real signs of replacing the old methods. Nor do struggling education and finance committees show much sympathy to requests for specialist staff and equipment to enable radical changes to be made. So far most of us are at the primitive stage where we can do little more than look at some of the basic techniques, perhaps with an eye to the future, or perhaps with the aim of introducing our own fallible human minds to some processes and categories of thought that may in themselves help us to organize our intuitions.

One obvious example is the basic team approach of OR, the notion of collecting together different skills for an attack on a problem: if one does not work another might. This goes beyond mere co-operation to the recognition that assumptions are the enemy in decision-making. Another is the isomorphic model, either a mathematical or statistical one or an exercise in simulation. Even if the administrator stops short of using mathematics to settle intangibles there are plenty of smaller objective questions within the working of his own office where he can try his hand. Perhaps Monte Carlo can replace hunch in measuring random events, like telephone calls, which take up staff time: perhaps queueing theory can help in charting the need for service against available staff resources. Linear programming may be valuable in solving allocation problems, or those of routing, sequence or search. Network analysis is already beginning to be used, co-ordinating a number of techniques to plan and schedule a complicated non-repetitive process such as planning a new building.

Computers

Central and local government are increasingly using computers, though probably not as effectively as they might. Often the treasurer's records or routine pay calculations are as far as it goes. Administrators live in increasing fear of being replaced by computers but know astonishingly little about them: the chances are that they will tend to be taken over not by the computers but by the men who control them. There are signs already of what this can mean:

that the policy-making process has to fit into the computer's programme, because of a superficial notion of tidiness or economy. Of course there are many things that can just as well be done in a way that suits the machines, and so they ought to be fitted in, but the administrator should be clear about which is the tail and which is the dog.

Computers have two separate functions: one is high-speed arithmetical calculation and the other is data-processing—storing, sorting and ordering information, alphabetical as well as numerical.

The routine repetitive tasks in offices are ideally suited to their talents and since the first punch-card machines there has been a steady movement towards replacing clerks by machines. (It is interesting that they do not seem to have reduced the number, which grows annually, but they have prevented a still greater increase and, of course, greatly added to the speed of operations.) Half the computers now in use are doing clerical work, particularly on payroll operations, and before long can be expected to have removed most of the chores in office work.

But it is as an adjunct of operational research that computers are increasingly being considered. Any decision is likely to be the better for more up-to-date, carefully analysed, readily available information and computers can provide it. Many of the calculations required by the operational research scientist can clearly be done more effectively by a computer; the number of variables and limitations in a complex problem become more manageable particularly when they can be formulated in a way that allows a solution by linear programming. Most of these problems are solved by a process of approximation, successively narrowing down by trial and error: there is a good deal of repetitive arithmetic ready-made for a computer.

Where a problem can be quantified and expressed in mathematical terms then these methods are incontrovertibly useful. And many more problems can be quantified than we might superficially suppose. There is no harm in trying to quantify as much as possible, either, if the aim in doing so is to clear the ground—and the mind—for solution of the basic, philosophical, non-quantifiable questions by other means. If this leads to minimizing the importance of questions that cannot be quantified, however, then it is in the end a dangerous process, a recreation of the communications-machine, the classical bureaucracy in which deviation is the ultimate crime. The responsibility of the administrator is to keep in the forefront of his mind, and in the minds of his masters, the important issues and the less tangible, human aspects of them.

Research

The quest for hard information on the major, fundamental questions in education is usually associated with research but this rarely extends much beyond lip-service. Only about one-eighth of one per cent of the national educational budget is spent on research into any aspect of education. The amount LEAs spend is not recorded, but its impact is imperceptible.

Nationally the way research is handled is depressing. Some of the reasons are connected with democracy. Government action with regard to research on any major issue is bound to be fraught with hazards, for interpretation of any results is likely to be thought politically biased. Politics apart, the laboratory conditions necessary for objective assessment are normally unobtainable on anything of importance in education; even if they were obtained they would be thought to invalidate any findings by being unnatural. There are too many variables.

Until recently commissioning advisory council reports—with or without research—and sponsoring a few individual projects through the Department of Education and Science was as far as the government felt able to go as a direct agency. The Schools Council—already responsible for half the national expenditure on research—shows how the government has to work: the responsibility is vested in a working relationship between practising teachers, Her Majesty's Inspectors and a few local administrators.

Responsibility for national research is in practice divided between small official, semi-official and independent bodies, augmented by the individual efforts of universities, colleges of education and a few LEAs. Teachers themselves lack time and resources for anything other than sporadic and highly personal efforts. Even when they are given the resources to band together for collective action—for instance, in the new curriculum development centres inspired by the Schools Council—they may lack the expertise to tackle major issues of the kind likely to affect whole sectors of the education service.

In many ways the local education authorities are best placed to organize research. Theirs is the legal responsibility for the pattern of education in their areas. They too lack resources, because of the pressure of other commitments, and with a system of financial support from the government that sets no money aside for education let alone for educational research, the immediate prospects are not bright. Yet it is worth considering whether even if finance were available the LEAs would find the prospect of undertaking large scale research attractive.

The administrator and the researcher are not natural allies: the one considers himself in touch with reality and is suspicious of academic exercises that at best seem to tell him things he has known all along; the other may be too fearful of loss of integrity to choose subjects and methods of presentation useful to working officials. The important issues make valid research a difficult proposition. The service is, first of all, concerned with people and research involving human factors is likely to miss out a good deal of what in the end is important. Secondly changes are likely to have to come gradually if at all: individual children are being educated in schools so that any change is a potential threat to their well-being. Third, education is not merely in contact with the public but surrounded by it: parents' anxiety is always—rightly—for their own children not for theories. Fourth, the results of changes in educational systems and practices only show themselves, if at all, many years after their initiation, which is a poor proposition for a researcher intent on showing that his findings will give results. In twenty years so many other factors will have influenced any situation that it is virtually impossible to ascribe any consequences exclusively or even mainly to specific causes.

In the event, the kind of research that is undertaken does not always impress the administrator with its potential value as a major force for social improvement. 'Patterns of hitch-hiking on the Continent' may in fact be a subject likely to throw light on matters of more general social significance, but as a request from a university lecturer to be allowed to ask school children to write essays about their holidays it did not seem—to one administrator at least—a good bet. The rarefied atmosphere in which much university research is undertaken may well irritate rather than impress the teacher and administrator. Apparently bizarre topics, no feedback, overlap of activities between university departments, and worst of all, frequent requests to use children and neighbourhoods as guinea pigs—these are no doubt distorted impressions of the true picture but they are the impressions of many practitioners.

It is easy to agree that present research is inadequate, ill-co-ordinated and often ill-conceived. We may perhaps also agree that however far short of presenting a full picture the limited processes of research may fall in the most important matters with which the education service is concerned, nevertheless soundly-based enquiry and carefully argued conclusions can be of inestimable value and are indeed essential if we are to avoid prejudice, whims and hunches as the mainspring of action. Finally we may agree that the local education authorities should organize the disciplined purposeful yet independent research that is needed so that accepted findings can have a chance of being put into practice. It is not so easy to suggest how.

The first essential is that LEAs should acknowledge the potential value of research as a basis for reasoned consideration of possible innovation and, equally important, as continuing evaluation of existing practices. This involves more than setting aside funds for research, though that is stage one: it means an office organization sensitive to the possibilities and capable of getting value for money out of the research.

A second development, without which the first may be much less useful, is to stimulate and facilitate the organization of practising teachers (together with advisers and administrators) to play a part in research activities. Their own enquiries, collectively undertaken, may be of value in themselves and they should do something to encourage teachers to see the potential of research as a practical working tool. As a corollary this collaboration could help to ensure that the topics considered by practitioners to need investigation were in fact covered, to inject reality into the process.

The third possibility stems directly from this—links between local universities, colleges of education and other higher education institutions, and the organized teacher-groups. These links could at the same time provide the expertise and guidance in research methods without which enthusiasm can be wasted effort and help university researchers by confronting them with the real issues in education as their teacher colleagues see them.

All this must be dependent to some extent on chance. Authorities, as a fourth possibility, might also consider commissioning research projects of their own to deal with specific problems of concern to them. Both from the point of view of economy and of avoiding fragmentation through separate unco-ordinated approaches they might consider doing this through their national body, the Association of Education Committees, or through a regional consultative committee. A collective approach like this would also emphasize that knowledge, above all things, increases its value when it is shared.

This last point in turn emphasizes that however well-organized the research, or the information-collection system generally, its value must be minimal unless the results are communicated effectively to those likely to be able to use it. In the next chapter we turn to consider communication as yet another important administrative technique for the education officer.

11

Communication

The administrator is not a general leading assaults or an engineer designing a bridge. His world is one of words; even his occasional deeds are expressed in words. This is one reason why his job looks so easy but in fact ranges between the very unlikely and the completely impossible. For language is man's most highly developed means of communication and it can conceal, as well as convey, information. Coupled with memory, unreliable and highly selective, it can wreak havoc in a flash and pave the road of good intentions with brimstone tiles. It is a powerful but uncertain force that must be harnessed, and on the success of this operation the whole success of the enterprise may depend.

Who should be told what, is a question so plaguing to the administrator that he tends to push it to the back of his mind. In the public service it is possible to find systems in which everyone is told everything (fifty copies of every document) and systems in which nobody is told anything (they read about it in the local paper). At the receiving end people may complain either that they are deluged with paper or that they are kept in the dark. It is a contemporary cliché by now that the more complex the organization grows the more difficult communication becomes. Internal communications themselves are to be found in triplicate; downwards, sideways and upwards : the means as well as the manner may cause difficulties. External communications have their own hazards. Both internally and externally there is invariably an informal network as well as the formal one. There is a fundamental tension between the written and the spoken word : the one more burdensome to produce and more binding; the other easier but with its own brand of treachery.

The proper channels

Uncertainty about roles, responsibilities and relationships can lead to poor communications: poor communications can cause uncertainty about roles, responsibilities and relationships. There is no more vicious circle. The structure and working principles of the organization need to be matched with the communications system. This ought to be one of the most resounding platitudes ever uttered but the chances are that whatever the structure of the organization, written communication will follow the hierarchical down-and-up-the-line pattern and that this will be found a cumbersome, prolonged and ineffective method—ready-made in fact for being by-passed. The hierarchical system is frequently a means of passing paper through many pairs of hands without substantial contribution to, or action on, whatever the paper contains. A more realistic organization can eliminate a lot of unnecessary sources of delay provided the communication-lines are redrawn to match.

We are discussing of course, operational communications, designed to precipitate, or to give effect to, a decision. Communication for information can follow the same route though it may be a source of confusion if it does. The operational line runs, metaphorically at any rate, vertically and the information line laterally. For operational effectiveness the fewer stages the better (for speed, avoiding distortion of the message or discouraging the men at either end of the line). Every stage should contribute something or be eliminated.

As a simple example we may take a memorandum in the chain Legree-Middleman-Drudge. If the true operational line is Legree-Drudge the main line of communication should be Legree-Drudge. To include Middleman may take longer, allow unnecessary opportunity for further delay (through absence or misdirection), irritate Drudge by the second-hand nature of the message, and confuse Middleman (is he entitled, or even expected, to modify the message: has he any standing or responsibility in the matter?). A better way is a message Legree-Drudge with a copy to Middleman for information. The alternative is a message Legree-Middleman leaving Middleman to take action himself or to get someone else—perhaps but not necessarily Drudge. Which way is chosen should depend on the nature of the transaction and on the operational roles of Middleman and Drudge. The temptation is, if Middleman is Drudge's hierarchical (but not, on this occasion, operational) superior, to include him in the chain of communication largely for the purpose of satisfying the proprieties and keeping him informed.

In operational communication from the top the main problems tend to be failure to realize that a decision has to be communicated, failure to despatch it to the right place, failure to get the message across properly. The first failure is one of those matters so simple that it is tremendously hard: taking thought, making time and just plain remembering are not as easy as they sound. The second we will hope can be cleared up by analysis of structure and relationships. The third is potentially much more troublesome because its deficiencies may not be easily apparent. Most people communicate as well as they know how: to express a message to those concerned in language they are likely to understand requires perception and skill.

Upward communication has the twin purpose of informing the men at the top properly and involving the men lower down. If the organization is ever to change at all there has to be a free flow in this direction. Once again the middle men have an ambiguous role: they are needed to screen the top men from trivia or poor ideas, but can be a nuisance if they have the not unknown tendency to want to appear to the boss as the ideas-men themselves. In an acute form this can mean that no idea is a good one unless they have it. An occasional informal session at which bright young men can try out their notions is one way round the difficulty, and an open atmosphere of pooling ideas and sharing problems is essential. The kind of organization that does not depend too much on the hierarchical pattern not only simplifies and shortens the actual line of communication but helps to create the right atmosphere.

Communication sideways is not merely a matter of keeping everyone in the picture, important as that is: it is a major factor in co-ordination. The more complex the organization, the more operational groups it has, the more the hinge of co-ordination is needed. And, of course, public administration itself, overlapping departmentally, criss-crossing between central, regional and local agencies, inter-weaving with statutory and voluntary activities, grows more complex and in need of co-ordination every day. No one has even begun to solve the problem: co-ordinating committees are a favourite device and generally a source of still greater confusion through over-elaboration. Freedom of movement to collaborate and communicate at the critical points of operation looks a better bet.

The fewer the stages in the vertical communication system and the less the need for messages to travel up the line before crossing to go down again, the better lateral communication is likely to be.

The informal network

Informal organizations tend to be set up within any formal structure. Most of the studies of this phenomenon have been with industrial workers : much less has been done with management and little if anything with administrators. In worker-groups the trend is towards co-operation, conservatism and avoidance of limelight by the individual. In management circles there may be more competition, orientation towards change and desire to be noticed. In both cases if the formal hierarchy does not work it will at critical moments tend to be side-stepped and the real leaders may take over.

The informal communications network is, of course, related to this. The official system may fail to work because it follows formal patterns that are out of line with practicalities, or because it does not deal with matters that are considered important. Conversely where there is an effective communications link over certain matters these things tend to assume a greater importance.

The gap between formal and informal communications networks is usually better bridged by bringing the formal system nearer to the natural one than attempting to stamp out the underground movement. The natural system may be merely a habit that is easy or unreflecting : if so it should be possible by patient explanation of the purpose and value of the official network to make sure it is used. Surprisingly often a confrontation of this kind may show, however, that the orthodox approach is just something traditional or theoretical and that it can safely be scrapped.

The formal and the informal tend to divide themselves into the written and the oral. Word of mouth, abetted by the telephone, is on the face of it easier, and the two-way traffic it allows has a special value. The division is not entirely one of means, however : departments may well augment—or replace—official communication by 'semi-official' or 'personal' letters. In local government where the convention is for all correspondence to be addressed to and 'signed' by the chief officer there is often a need for this : if a member of staff has dealings with an architect or a member of the public it will seem natural to them to write to him direct. In central government the intention is to give an informal opinion or piece of advice without committing the department. This kind of deviation has a purpose. A more serious departure is of the kind that seeks to do the job of the formal system better and by creating confusion or clogging up the works in fact makes matters worse.

The filing system

It is worth looking at the filing system as an example of the problem, partly because it is neglected territory and partly because of its position at the centre of the network of communication and information within the organization and the effect it can have on external communications. The filing system is often the office joke, and heaven knows a lot of offices need a joke, but filing can be an expensive way of amusement: it can bring the office to its knees.

We need spend little time on the hardware, though good equipment can make a difference not least in showing how seriously the business is taken. Those old-fashioned pull-out metal drawers take up a lot of space and are really more useful for storing teapots or knitting. Lateral systems need less room and make identification, and therefore an organized system, easier. But there are also revolving systems, mechanized filing and microfilm: a good consultant is the answer.

The real concern is with the system and the way it is run. In many offices it is given out to the feeblest member of staff and apart from cursing, the senior staff play no part in it. No one suggests that it is a top job—though it is possible to learn a lot about an office by its filing system—but some thought by those it serves will pay dividends. Otherwise private filing systems, duplicating, or worse making holes in, the official system, spring up like mushrooms. The system has to store documents away without difficulty and produce them in a convenient form on demand. If it fails then there are bound to be pirates.

The size and complexity of the department may point to one central or a number of separate locations. A decentralized system need not mean anarchy, nor need a centralized one impose a rigid pattern on all branches. A logical and flexible pattern outlined in a central register with appropriate variations on the theme in the outposts will serve most purposes, especially if there are named filing clerks in each branch co-ordinated by someone with overall responsibility. The pattern chosen makes no difference—alphabetical, topical, chronological or an amalgam—provided it is understood by everybody. The simpler the system the easier it will be to label the documents correctly and if it can be based on needs arising from the job there will rarely be any trouble.

Unless it is a simple and logical system there can quickly be too many different files, so that a document could reasonably be on any one of a dozen files. On the other hand files that are too general make it hard to find anything without a half-hour search and increase the chance of somebody else having it when it is wanted. The volume of filing is best reduced by distinguishing between current files and records, stored elsewhere, perhaps on microfilm.

Adaptation to working needs rather than doctrinaire principles is more likely to preserve the value of the official system and encourage its use. Thus although one place only for everything is not a bad rule, some things may need to be handy in two or three different places at once—a file on office procedures for instance—and it is better to provide them than infuriate everyone or encourage small private collections of miscellaneous useful information. Even the private collection itself may be admissible—for instance for confidential reasons—and if its location is recorded in the central book no one need worry that if Buggins gets sciatica the job will have to stop.

A pragmatic approach

To allow into the filing system things which have a useful purpose even though pure theory would exclude them, is an aspect of coming to terms with the informal, natural communications system as a whole. Text-books on communications that start with cold, clear principles to be deduced and then implemented may unwittingly do a disservice in more ways than one. First, they are likely to fall to the ground because of the essentially pragmatic, intuitive way people in the end communicate. But second, and ultimately more important, however vital communications are they cannot safely be elevated to the point of front-line activities such as thought. Outside administration the dangers of the mass-media taking over are plain to see: within it the communications-machine can so easily begin to operate for its own sake, as an art in itself.

This is not to say that there should never be a long, cool look at the way communications work and a systematic attempt to improve them. It is simply to suggest that there can be few principles of sufficiently general application to be any use. What is the criterion: speed, accuracy, sympathy, economy, harmonious staff relations? Often these are mutually exclusive qualities in the circumstances in which they arise. Philosophy of work, policy decisions, an organization to match, methods of working in line with them all—these must come first and the communications system must be the kind which helps them most.

In the same way it seems unwise to be doctrinaire about whether to emphasize written or oral communication. Telephoning may often be a synonym for wasting time and being telephoned an invitation to forget: the exercise of writing it down may be a fine way to clear the mind and to keep a record; but a brief talk may achieve more than mountains of memoranda. It all depends on the purpose.

Decisions on policy need a written commentary even though they may be reached in a face-to-face encounter. Clearly stated, carefully recorded, frequently revised policy statements are one of the most important pieces of administrative machinery. Local authorities have a head start with the fully recorded minutes of committee meetings and the practice is worth extending to any meeting, even an internal office session, at which policy decisions are likely to be taken. There is no evidence that spontaneity and inspiration are in any way limited by recording what has been said (provided it really ought to have been said). On the other hand there is increasing evidence of the ill-temper that faulty recollection, unofficial attribution and second-hand opinions can cause.

Consultation

Nothing is achieved, in the late twentieth century, without consultation. Nothing causes more trouble, whether it takes place or whether it is neglected. Any discussion of consultation really needs to be an assessment of the balance of disadvantages, for the only fruitful conclusion is that horrible as its effects may be, it is worse not to consult than to do it.

Let us consider first the hazards. An early problem is remembering to do it at all. Remembering anything is difficult; and one of the hardest things we have to do is to remember in advance that, in the event of something happening, we have to take a certain course of action. All we can do is to formulate organized procedures, lay down a drill in writing in advance and set up the machinery for doing it. What tends to happen is that, once a particular episode is over, we drop it at once, perhaps in relief, certainly to turn to some new pressing problem. Yet the moment to formulate our plans for next time is just then, when the episode, mistakes and all, is fresh in the mind.

Remembering to consult has extra snags. Failure to consult is often the result of simple forgetfulness: it is certainly rarely deliberate. Yet it may not be wholly free from the taint of Freudian lapses of memory—the things we forget because we don't want to remember. Since acquiring a taste for consultation is an unlikely contingency this is all the more reason for organizing the procedure for it in advance.

One interesting phenomenon has to be recorded, death by consultation. This is a process, well known to administrators, in which, landed with a decision you do not much like yet fearful or powerless to challenge it, you simply consult, fully and with due deliberation, everyone who is in any way concerned. The result spells death to the project, or at least leads to substantial and useful delay. Such a disreputable approach is out of place in this high-minded volume, though it points to yet more problems of consultation.

Who is entitled to be consulted? Is it simply a question of the more the better? Because, of course, a central difficulty is that those who are consulted tend to think that their own views ought to be accepted: otherwise they say, what is the use of consulting us? Their complaints may indeed be even louder than if they had never been asked. The horns of this particular dilemma are very sharp and spiky. There is no answer to it, and perhaps only one small palliative. That is to make it clear from the outset what stage has been reached in the decision-making process; what other factors have to be taken into account; what your own view is; and how far you accept what the consulted have to say.

Another key question is at what stage to consult. Education officers are often consulting on behalf of their committees, who may have the power of final decision. If they consult before they are sure of the committee's views it may at best be a waste of time and at worst a risk of reaching an agreement that cannot subsequently be honoured. On the other hand, if a decision is taken or even half-taken in advance, then they are likely to be accused of presenting a *fait accompli.*

Of the two the second is undoubtedly the worse. There is nothing more embarrassing or shabby than to have to consult someone when the die is already cast, whether they know it or not: there is nothing more insulting or infuriating to those being consulted. The honourable and the prudent course is to clear the ground beforehand, to consider possibilities and even to prepare plans, but to go into the consultation with an open mind or at least the possibility of more than one course of action.

There is a kind of consultation that quite legitimately consists of explaining policy after it is agreed, but before it is implemented. It would be impractical to consult the public in advance. Yet we have a duty, often sadly neglected, to explain, fully and in good time. More than a little disillusionment often results for the well-meaning administrator who innocently supposes that once the logic of a decision is explained all will be well. An unenthusiastic or hostile reception may mean that the plan is a bad one : on the other hand it may not, and in any case the plan may have to be implemented. What it clearly does mean is that more explanation is needed.

It is worth remembering that Englishmen usually need telling twice. It is amazing too what a difference allowing a decent interval to elapse can have. All the clichés—tempers are allowed to cool, wiser counsels prevail, time is the great healer—are quite true. And so sometimes is the one about more haste, less speed, as many authorities rushing at breakneck speed into progressive new policies have discovered. The timing of this type of consultation is important. Even though the proposal being made is entirely reasonable, with perhaps a good chance of being accepted, everything can be ruined by poor timing. People don't like to be taken for granted.

Public relations

A good deal of communication is involuntary. The Press and the television networks are so highly organized, so avid for news, that whether we like it or not the public service is public knowledge. Most administrators don't like it. Opinion as to why this is so probably depends on where you sit. The Press and public think it is because bureaucrats like to keep their decisions and their mistakes secret : the bureaucrats think it is because they almost always are misrepresented. Perhaps the popular view is right : certainly as long as officials are expected to be infallible their main aim will be the avoidance of error and they will want to play things pretty close to their chests. On the other hand there are many occasions when a desire to shock and scandalize seems to distort the facts, and even more times when sheer ignorance of complex or technical matters leads reporters into error.

There are still some administrators who react to this by withdrawing all voluntary contact with the mass media. It is doubtful whether as public servants they are always entitled to do this. In any event they cannot avoid the involuntary contact their service has with press, radio and television. Co-operation may lead to disillusionment (since bad news seems to have more appeal than good, and corruption and ineptitude are more interesting than beautifully executed plans) but the mass media are natural means of communication which cannot be ignored.

A particular hazard is the sudden news story, the urgent telephone call wanting a comment on some national or local development. 'No comment' in these circumstances can be just as bad as a garbled misquotation. It helps to try to anticipate these requests—for example when a new national report comes out it is a safe bet that the local press will want to know what its effect is likely to be— by having a statement prepared in advance. Otherwise it is generally better to offer to ring back : it is worth the cost of the telephone call to have the story right before plunging in.

But true public relations is more positive : it involves as much contact with the public as possible. It involves trying to consult and explain in advance, presenting policies openly, by official bulletins, by public meetings, through accepted channels (groups like trades unions, chambers of trade and commerce, civic societies, Rotary and Round Table, Women's Institutes, Townswomen's Guilds and parent-teacher associations). The education officer needs to take every opportunity to appear in public; for example, when he is asked to speak or attend a function, such as a reception or a school prize-giving, and to identify himself as much as possible with the community he serves.

The advent of local radio in some areas provides a new opportunity for a positive approach to communication. Here is an ideal medium for confrontation between administrator and public, an opportunity to explain policies, a means of allaying anxieties and answering questions of general concern.

Basic communications

The point at which clear, effective communication is day in, day out of most importance is in the fundamental practice of a basic skill—the writing of letters and memoranda.

Senior administrators have a threefold responsibility in this. First, they must take infinite pains with the written material they themselves produce, both to get results and to set an example to those they lead. Unless the top men care about the structure and texture of what they themselves produce then they will wait in vain for their subordinates to produce ready-made material of the right standard. Second, they must pay great—and personal—attention to the training of staff in this basic activity. The third responsibility is an extension of the second. Officers coming into a department are entitled to know in advance what is expected of them : they should not be simply left to their own devices and then criticized afterwards. An office guide on procedures and practice is essential in any large organization. Apart from the intrinsic value, producing such a guide can help to clarify objectives and uncertainties for the compilers as well as the users. The need to consider in an organized way what to put before a committee or how to address the public can lead to consideration of a still more fundamental matter, the proper relationship between the administrator and those with whom he deals.

12

Relationships

Nowhere has the influence of sociology and social psychology been more keenly felt in recent years than in its emphasis on the concept of roles and relationships. It is fair to say that this has not so far been an entirely unmixed blessing, particularly when blunted by crude and self-centred interpretations. It can for example lead to a self-consciousness liable to kill all natural communication. It can sometimes seem to be no more than a vogue word, a label to be attached to a problem as a substitute for rather than an aid to solving it. To treat someone shabbily is no more commendable if it is described as an unsatisfactory relationship than if it is called a dirty trick.

Distortion does not make the potential value of the concept any less. One aspect of it indeed is particularly relevant to the administration of education. L. J. Westwood of the National Foundation for Educational Research in a recent article put it like this:

'The basic idea behind the concept of role is that all men can be seen to "play certain parts" in life—at different times and in differing circumstances. There are, to put it slightly differently, certain broad uniformities in human behaviour which are specific to particular social situations and relationships. Each individual plays many different roles; the same man may, for example, play the role of teacher, father, husband and chairman of a committee—perhaps all on the same day—and will almost certainly behave in essentially different ways when playing each role.'

Relationships

In administration generally there is it seems an almost universal search for a generalized, fixed definition of individual roles. In part it is a quest for security and stability in an uncertain world; in part a quest for status. However understandable this may be it is almost entirely inimical to constructive working. Of course people need to know 'where they stand' and what their functions are. There are certain built-in expectations. Westwood goes on:

> 'Within each role, however, he will be behaving in ways which conform, broadly, to the conceptions that others have as to how an individual performing this role (usually termed the role incumbent) will behave; in other words, there will always be a certain degree of predictability about the behaviour of any role incumbent. Indeed there must be, since without such predictability, social organization in both larger and smaller social systems would be impossible.'

But any suggestion of general and definite fixed permanent relationships is unhelpful in all but the most bureaucratic organizations and therefore quite inappropriate in the education service.

The quality of the relationships of those engaged in education determines in large measure the quality of the education they are able to provide. So in the remaining chapters some aspects of the insubstantial and shifting relationships within education will be examined: first, in the administration itself.

A necessary pre-condition of education in our society is that it should be democratic. It may be agreed, therefore, that the government of the service should itself be democratic. As we have seen, there is no shortage of institutional democracy in education: it exists to the point, perhaps, of obscuring the objectives of the service. But such institutions are feeble instruments unless they are informed by a democratic spirit: that is to say unless the relationships they invoke are themselves democratic.

This does not mean, of course, that there should be no order; nor even that there should be no hierarchies. In an office the hierarchy has its necessary place, provided it does not attempt to ossify what should be flexible, and the same is true in the broader context of the education service generally. Nor does it mean merely that those working the system should try to avoid being starchy (although that helps). It relates rather to the acceptance by everyone in the service of the source and nature of their authority.

The various education acts have created a national system based not on an all-powerful central control with local functionaries, but on the notion of partnership. All the partners have their roles and those roles are not given to them by their partners but by the ultimate source of authority, Parliament and, thus, the people. This same notion can be applied to every relationship that arises from the myriad situations brought about by this basic legislation.

The notion is, of course, too ponderous and stultifying to apply directly to every facet of the service, but as an informing spirit it may perhaps clarify some of the problems. The Secretary of State, his Department, the LEA and its committees, governors and managers, teachers and parents all have their part to play, and although in particular circumstances there may be an apparent superior-inferior relationship this arises only from the legislative requirements of the Act: it is in fact invalidated if the object of the exercise is itself not what the Act intends.

The corollary of this is that relationships may change as circumstances change; which may make it easier to accept the sometimes bewildering interplay of relationships that may occur in education. The Chairman of a Board of Governors may also be a parent: his relationship to the education officer will change according to which role the particular circumstances require him to play. There may, of course, be some overspill from one role to the other, though it would be unfortunate if this went to the lengths of giving preferential treatment to the chairman (in the allocation of secondary school places for instance). Legitimate overspill is the realistic acceptance that relationships change (normally though not always for the better) when people know each other.

Within the office

Within the education office it might perhaps be thought that traditional local government hierarchical relationships would suffice. This begs the question of whether these concepts are in fact sufficient for local government generally. But apart from this there are tensions peculiar to education offices that call for something more imaginative. First there is the (sometimes significant) gap between those coming into the office from teaching and those coming up through local government channels, normally having started in the Town or County Hall straight from school. Second, there is a very wide range of different disciplines covered by educational administration. Third, there is often a substantial difference of outlook between advisers and administrators.

The tensions arising from these differing outlooks can create acute problems of relationship within the office. And the need for education to be a dynamic not a static service reinforces the desirability of flexibility and variation in relationships within the administrative structure.

It was suggested in Chapter Five that a hierarchical ladder was of less value as a model of working methods than a cluster of cells with short, operational lines of command and communication, clusters that form and re-form according to the particular task to be performed. The design of a school may require temporarily the combined forces of a number of people who are normally attached to other sections of the office than the special branch dealing with sites and buildings. An organized team of those involved on the project, each with a clear idea of his function on the job, may not only be the most efficient approach but the one most likely to be satisfying to those taking part.

The team is a form of organization that men appear to create naturally, both for work and for play. Nor does it seem, in sport, to have lost any of its appeal as society has grown more complex : quite the contrary. Traditionally, it has a special appeal for the British : it is not too fanciful therefore to see in it great possibilities for dealing with the characteristically British complex of compromises embedded in the education system. The basis of the team is collective action through the willing subordination of individuals to the general good. With its emphasis on inter-dependence it is the essence of democracy, and its essential process of creating a whole that is greater than the sum of its individual parts seems well-suited to making democracy efficient.

Teams assemble for a purpose and are disbanded afterwards. Their function is limited to particular ends. This contrasts with the notion of institutions—such as education offices—with a permanent structure, rather general objectives, and a static organization. Yet the tasks to be performed by the institutions are ever-changing. Some aspects of the institutions are necessary to preserve order and stability : in any event the traditional structures are likely to remain, and we must work within the realities. The team idea can be used to provide the dynamism needed to animate the institutions, not by challenging their existence, but by strengthening them.

Officers and members

The committee situation is one in which relationships between officers and members are of over-riding importance. One of the proposals of the Maud Report referred to in Chapter 9, was that elected members should deal only with policy issues and should delegate specific examples of them to paid officials. This has led to spirited controversy about the relationship between committees and their officers and most attention has been given to the difficulty of building up policies except through specific examples. A more fundamental weakness of the Report's idea, however, may be that it is seeking a generalized, universal solution whereas the 'relationship' between officers and members is in fact a collection of different, if related, relationships, changing according to the particular task in hand. The connotations of stereotypes such as 'members and officers' and even 'committee' are likely to have a stultifying effect: study of the particular job to be done comes first, before any generalizations about roles.

In education where decisions regularly concern philosophy as well as high finance, the conventional committee machinery shows its limitations more even than in other branches. Members are not in any sense involved in policy-making if in a complex and far-reaching matter their only function is to consider a report from an officer. They have, it is true, the unfettered right to say 'yes' or 'no', but this power is often more illusory than real. On a complicated issue much of the policy has in fact been determined once the report has been written: the approaches to the problem, the selection of facets within it, can settle in advance the lines of decision-making.

One way of progress is to break the stereotype. We have referred earlier to working parties to supplement the formal committee procedures. This is just one name for a form of organization that itself represents only one way of making headway. But it is a useful and practical example of what can be done, particularly in dealing with broad general questions of policy. The characteristics of the working party include informal, round-the-table discussion, without voting, without necessarily trying to settle specific issues, in advance of the formal committee meetings when actual policy decisions are taken. The base of membership can be broadened to include anyone with something to contribute; there need be no rigid adherence to an agenda, no limiting protocol about moving amendments or substantive motions. Above all they allow a relaxed, natural relationship between officers and members.

Perhaps on the surface the relaxation seems to confuse not clarify the relationship, but if it is accepted that 'the relationship' is not a helpful notion this is no real handicap. In effect they produce

171

a different, more appropriate relationship designed to allow elected members to play a real part in policy-making and to prevent officers from evading their responsibilities by sheltering behind the myth that members make decisions, officers merely carry them out. Since working parties are not normally standing committees, but are set up for particular purposes, they can be disbanded when their work is done. This is a clear example of the team situation at work : the members pool their resources during the meetings and collectively accept responsibility for policy. Afterwards, when the team function has ended, different relationships, relevant to the new situation, can come into being.

There may, of course, be overspill; but of a constructive kind. In practice the mutual respect and confidence built up in an informal situation free of stereotyped expectations about roles is likely to lead to an improvement in relationship in more formal situations later. The trust of members in their officer-colleagues is almost certain to increase if members are manifestly being brought in at the early stages of policy-formation, which must improve the chances of success of the member-policy, officer-execution theory advocated by Maud in the later formal committee stages.

Inter-professional team-work

Officers are too prone to blame the inadequacies of their services on the existence of committees. In education, we have agreed, committees are essential. Quite apart from the democratic safeguards they provide there is a very real sense in which their existence adds the flexibility necessary to a developing service and one concerned with people. On further education awards, for example, the local education authorities were usually more sensitive to the claims of individuals than the Department of Education and Science was with its State Scholarship scheme.

Relations between officers represents a problem at least equal to that of relations between officers and members. Individual offices may themselves be hide-bound and apparently immutable, and there are formidable difficulties between departments. Much energy that could more profitably be spent in the interests of the community goes instead into territorial struggles that can range from the negative and unhelpful to the positively hostile. Local authorities are acutely aware of these problems and the recent outcrop of solutions (following the Maud and Mallaby reports) in which Chief Executives and other overlords are appointed as co-ordinators is evidence of this.

These solutions must be given a chance but it is doubtful if in themselves they can achieve all that is necessary. One reason is that will cannot be replaced by machinery. Another is that most of the co-ordinating solutions are themselves conceived in static, generalized terms : additional centralized institutions may provide little more than fifth wheels to the coach even if they do not earn themselves a worse metaphor, bottlenecks. The same potential weakness seems to be built into the Seebohm Committee's proposals for a social service department to harness together all the many facets of local authority personal social services.

These proposals are intended to combat the increasing specialization that our institutions have developed in response to the needs over the years of different aspects of society. The machinery has grown more and more elaborate, sometimes over-sophisticated. Some of the consequent muddle is the result of the quirks of history, revealing fragments of social need at different times : some is the result of rapid social change. There is thus an undoubted need for overhaul. But it seems naïve to suppose that the increasingly complex problems we are and shall be able to detect can be solved by creating simple, centralized general institutions offering once-for-all solutions. It is more likely that the answer will emerge through making more effective use of specialization rather than trying to escape it : and that the best approach lies in dynamic rather than static solutions.

The team has already been suggested as an idea offering the necessary mobility and flexibility. It is also well able to cope with the problems of specialization. Specialization is, after all, a critical problem for teams, sporting and otherwise. If they do not specialize they may be unable to face the challenge of the opposition : if specialization gets out of hand the collective energy we call team spirit may be dissipated. In seeking to create this kind of team-spirit amongst specialists in local government most attention has been focused on co-ordinating the work of departments. The weakness of this is that in seeking to establish permanent cohesion it misses the point that teams operate only intermittently and *ad hoc*. Liaison should begin with the specialists themselves, who operate in the field, not the administrators.

The specialist, particularly the field-worker, needs a degree of freedom from bureaucracy : that will apply whether or not all the specialists are in one department or scattered amongst many. But he cannot be allowed—for all sorts of reasons—to operate entirely independently. The traditional method of limiting his activities is to provide him with a set of rules and require him to refer hard cases back to headquarters. In the education service alone many thousands of children have suffered because of this approach which inhibits the psychologist, the education welfare officer and their colleagues from taking swift action to deal with cases of educational handicap. The system also discourages co-operation between specialists, since each has his own administrative headquarters to which he owes first loyalty. It encourages on the other hand narrow sectional attitudes in the diagnosis of handicap, and allows the timid or lazy field-worker to shelter behind the regulations.

The first requirement, then, is for the administrator to set free specialists in his own sphere to co-operate with counterparts in other disciplines: this applies whether they are employed by different sections of the education office or different local government departments. Problems that might otherwise seem fantastically difficult, involving passing on administrative responsibility from one branch to another, can be resolved if each branch delegates responsibility to the field-worker, and allows him to work as part of a team.

The team work is of course an essential part of the exercise. The specialists in the field can band together for strength: if all relevant experts agree on a solution no one back at base is likely to be in a position to question the decision. Furthermore the exercise can become one of operational research, in which the various skills (and the contents of files) can be pooled. The problem can thus be looked at from all angles: it can simultaneously be seen as a whole and as potentially soluble by any one of several disciplines. One particular specialist can then be nominated to be responsible for the problem thereafter, and he can accept this responsibility knowing that he is going to be helped not hindered by the pressure of other experts.

First things first

To begin by looking at the education officer's relationships with his colleagues and his committees is perhaps to run the risk of introspection. Fiddling while Rome burns is bad enough, but contemplating one's own navel during the conflagration is even worse. And notions like 'the importance of relationships' can invite navel-contemplation and similar forms of unproductive self-consciousness.

The spirit in which we have looked first at these internal relationships is not, however, based on narcissism. It is rather that of putting one's own house in order before trying to reform the neighbourhood.

In the two remaining chapters we must try to get the matter in perspective by emphasizing that administration is not an end in itself. The relationships we now have to consider, first with the teachers, then with the community, should make this abundantly clear. Educational administration exists first to support the teachers so that they in turn can serve the people.

13

Education officers
and teachers

Educational administration exists in order to make good teaching possible. The adjective is an important qualification but it does not affect the basic point, that administration is service not mastery. When we consider the relationship between education officers and teachers that notion must provide the context. And if we describe the relationship as a partnership, and as a vital one for the future of education, we must be clear what we mean. Not a convenient arrangement in which front-line troops, necessary but expendable, are flung into battle, but a means of enabling professional educators to do their best for the nation's children.

It would be easy to over-simplify. The point has already been made that there are no static relationships in education. So, too, in this partnership. Roles change with time: a new assistant education officer will have a different relationship with a head already in post when he arrives from that of an experienced AEO with a newly appointed head. They change according to circumstances: the same head who last week asked for help with a case of drug-taking may next appear as a co-opted member of the education committee or as a representative of a teacher association.

This changing relationship is an important notion for a new administrator to cling to: there is no *one* right one, so there is no fixed ideal to be attained and no sense of failure or frustration if it is not. Instead there is a series of different situations in which each partner plays his part. We shall look at them, as we must, separately but there has to be in each set-piece recognition of the possibilities of change when the next one comes along.

Teachers as personnel

Selection and appointment

Franz Kafka could have produced a good book about the appointment of teachers in British schools and colleges. There is a thread of amateurish anarchy running through the process which seems at first sight to be the bizarre, accidental fruit of a casual and loveless union between academics, academics-turned-bureaucrat, and politicians. On closer examination it is the inevitable, though irrational, outcome of our concern for democratic safeguards, our belief that academic values and freedom are threatened by rationalized management. Add to this several score variations on the theme—different authorities, different methods for primary schools and colleges of further education—and the prospect of even describing what goes on is daunting. This attempt is stylized and omits all the 'ifs' 'buts' and 'elsewheres'.

Most teachers first encounter administrators when they apply for their first job: or at least they encounter the administrative machine. The confrontation may be made easier for both parties if the applicant is at a college of education where advice is given about the procedure and if the authority concerned goes to the trouble of sending information about itself and its procedures to the various colleges.

The main exercise of recruiting new teachers is conducted by agreement amongst authorities in a few days around Easter. It could be done better if it happened later when all resignations were in. As it is authorities have to appoint first and allocate to schools later. No one is—or ought to be—content to be posted to a school they haven't seen or to work for a head they haven't met. The system only works at all one suspects because large numbers of college students want to teach in their own home districts, or to go off together with friends to a district that seems congenial or an authority that acquires—justly or not—a good reputation over the years. Authorities take great care, within the limitations of the system, to find suitable first schools for the probationers, so it is usual to discuss possibilities with all the applicants at their interview to find out the type of school and district they prefer and to discover where they might fit in best, but to postpone decisions about a posting until all vacancies are known. Then there is a full-scale attempt to match up schools and candidates with, let us hope, the emphasis at this stage on choosing a suitable place for the new teacher to begin a career.

Properly used the method can work out to the advantage of the teacher : at the end of the probationer year he can feel free to move having perhaps made a few mistakes and make a fresh start elsewhere. Or he can be interviewed by the managers and appointed to the permanent staff if all has gone well. The more usual method in secondary schools, where particular subjects are involved, of filling posts only where vacancies already exist places a greater onus on the teacher himself to be sure that the school is the right one for him.

It is difficult to measure success in this operation. If the supply position is bad, success may mean no more than filling the gaps, but most people would hope to do better than that. Supply and demand, and judgement in the actual placing, are the dominant factors but the organization of the exercise can significantly affect it. It has to begin as soon as the previous year's allocation has ended. Instead of sighs of relief there has to be a conference of everyone who has been involved : the record of events (which we assume has been carefully kept) is examined and adjustments suggested for the following year. The distribution of applications, by colleges, age-ranges and subjects, is analysed and the strategy of advertisement adjusted. The preparation and revision of written material, application forms, handbooks for applicants, and publicity material is better looked at in the immediate aftermath than hurriedly just before next time round.

Few colleges and university departments of education find much time in their courses for instruction in the theory and practice of applying for jobs. Yet it is knowledge that teachers will need throughout their careers, particularly when they begin to apply for more senior posts, short-lists are drawn up and competitive interviews held. There are both ethical and practical considerations, for instance, in accepting a post and subsequently withdrawing, and not all candidates appear to realize that they will normally be expected to say 'yes' or 'no' on the spot to an offer of a particular job. The sheer mechanics and etiquette of completing forms and writing accompanying letters evidently defeat many candidates. How many jobs have been lost through failure to write in more than the barest facts or conversely through sending pounds of additional material? And what of the people who, instead of filling in the form, send a mass-produced, all-purpose *curriculum vitae* that suggests that (*a*) they think nothing of the official form (*b*) they

178

know what potential employers want to know better than the employers know themselves and worst of all (*c*) they are unsuccessfully hawking themselves around? Yet most teachers have to rely on native wit, folk-lore or one of the desperately facetious and anecdotal books about how to get to the top. Authorities could help teachers and themselves in this. It would be a well-attended week-end course, one suspects, if the topics included the techniques, aims and etiquette of seeking promotion.

For the most part teachers are appointed by laymen. Apart from our fears of trampling on academic freedom, this has something to do with fear of corruption, and a good deal to do with history. Whatever the reasons most education committee members and boards of governors enjoy appointing teachers and take the job very seriously. There are some who would—and some who do—leave the appointment of asistant teachers entirely to heads on the grounds that any manager should have the right to appoint his own staff. Not all heads want this responsibility; nor do all teachers think heads should have it. The arguments are nicely balanced, and though personal opinion might support the managerial view, in practice informal arrangements in which a small group of governors join with the head can work very well. In colleges and bigger schools appointments by boards including members of staff are now being tried. Again, provided the exercise is organized carefully, someone present is skilled in interviewing and the job specification and candidate-requirements are well prepared, the system can benefit from different opinions.

Heads and principals are usually appointed by governors, supplemented perhaps by education committee members, or by a joint body. The group is likely to be large and to meet rarely. There is less opportunity for a familiar and useful technique to be evolved so that the education officer has to try to make up for the deficiencies. The extent of his influence will depend ultimately on the confidence the members have in his judgement, but he can help to build up this confidence by thorough and systematic attention to the processes of appointment.

Normally he will be able to design the application form, job analysis and candidate requirement sheets, advertisements and further particulars. The short-listing may be left to him. If not he must persuade the committee to consider carefully the criteria they need to employ and to have them agreed before selection begins. In any event he will have access to confidential references (which should surely be taken up before the short-list is prepared) and will know what to look for from the application forms. He will be able to arrange for candidates to visit the school before the interview and perhaps to see them himself informally then. He will have the opportunity of asking as many questions as he wants at the formal interview—this can be a crucial stage of the operation. More than anyone present he will be able to weigh the true merits of local candidates compared with outsiders. And, perhaps most important of all, he will be able to draw out the salient points about the candidates after they have been interviewed and when the committee's minds may still be reeling from the impact of hundreds of words. His job is not to choose, but to give his best advice and, equally important, his best assistance with the techniques of selection.

So the relationship between teacher and officer is complex in this first category. The education officer can be an important influence in the aspiring teacher's career, though not perhaps in the same way that some people think. He will, of course, meet some teachers many times on this sort of occasion. He will be anxious to see that good service and experience are rewarded, but will have to take particular care that each appointment is complete in itself and not a re-running of an earlier race with first prize tending to go to last time's runner-up.

The quality of education

We have referred already to the education officer's special responsibility to probationer teachers. This is part of his general concern for the quality of teaching. Much of his influence is exercised indirectly: through advisers, through administrative and financial support for experiment, through in-service training, through imaginative planning of buildings, through reorganization that is educationally stimulating. Most of his contact with schools and colleges is through heads and principals and his influence depends on his ability to inspire, to arouse enthusiasm for the authority's schemes.

It is sometimes considered polite to talk as though all heads were first-class and without blemish. They are not, just as education officers are not. The possibility of doing much about mediocrity is remote, bearing in mind the complex, diffuse nature of authority in education and the difficulty of measuring results. Example, that is contact with colleagues with higher standards, is the main hope. Another ray of hope is in the likelihood that there will be some aspects of the job at which even a generally mediocre performer will be good or better. This is, if you like, a mild version of the operational research approach: trying to find an angle from which the problem can be solved. Perhaps it will be new curriculum developments, management, parental relations, creating a happy school or even athletic prowess. To be good at something is to have a satisfying role and this can be the start of all-round improvement.

For the most part heads are very good at their jobs, much better than the environment in which they have to work, and the administrator will spend much of his time trying to see that administrative support matches the quality of the education. He is most unlikely to make the mistake of seeking to improve by introducing more control and direction. Thus the President of the Association of Chief Education Officers, Dr. J. J. B. Dempster in 1968 '. . . we feel that the freedom of the teacher and the independence of the school are important elements in education in this country and characteristics that we want to see enhanced rather than depressed by the changes that are going on at the moment. . . .'

Communications

The two-way exchange of information and consultation between the office and the institutions is the life-line of the education service, but we can too readily assume that good communications solve all problems. What is being communicated has its importance, too, and it is doubtful if unpalatable information becomes palatable through being smoothly transmitted. Perhaps bad news conveyed quickly does less harm: for example if an application for leave of absence to go on a course is declined it is better to tell the applicant some time before the day he is due to set off. On the other hand, rejections that come back with the speed of a bullet may suggest inadequate and unsympathetic consideration. Speed in the last resort is less important than effective handling.

The education office—schools situation is a classic opportunity for bad communications: one central base and a large number of outposts, with a number of built-in hazards such as committee and governors' meetings. It takes time for a stimulus to travel from the perimeter to the centre, more time for a decision to be reached and still more for the reply to be sent. By the time it gets back to the perimeter the circumstances may have changed. This can lead to annoyance and frustration which makes the prospects worse for next time: if the official channels are suspect unofficial ones are started which eventually by-pass the official ones and clog up the works.

Education officers and teachers

Poor communications can arise because someone does not wish to communicate, or through sloth. More often delays have an explanation but no one has thought to give it. Perhaps if teachers were told in advance what procedures had to be followed, and why, they would not assume incompetence or malignity or both. What steps are taken to tell the schools about procedure—for instance, applying for leave of absence? How often are important circulars reissued for the benefit of newcomers, both in the schools and in the office? If there is a regular bulletin are enough copies sent to make sure that every teacher has a chance to see one? Do teachers have an organization chart of headquarters staff so that they know whom to telephone? When information is sought from schools are they told why it is wanted? Is a time limit stated and is it a reasonable one?

Uncertainty about roles and relationships is always an invitation to poor communications, and there are many opportunities for uncertainty in such a complex network. If something goes wrong whom should I tell? When education offices present such an impenetrable front human contact is all important: when advisers visit schools they may carry with them much more than advice; they represent the office itself. So it is doubly important that advisers themselves are kept in touch with what's what on the administrative side.

Working relationships

Operational working

Teachers look to administrators for information, rulings, help and advice. Sometimes they want factual information; sometimes they just need to discuss a problem with someone who may have experience of similar difficulties before; sometimes it is a matter of interpreting the law or a regulation. The transaction may have the characteristics of consulting a solicitor, or a bank manager. A troublesome pupil may be stepping outside the bounds of normal school discipline, or a troublesome caretaker may be making life impossible.

The range of topics on which letters are sent or telephone calls made is almost limitless. It is two-way traffic and many heads may feel themselves subjected to a regular bombardment of requests for statistical information, invitations to courses, new staffing formulae, procedures for medical inspections and enquiries about teachers who are applying for posts in other authorities.

The relationship is correspondingly variable. Take head A and administrator B. A and B are colleagues. B advises A. A and B serve together on a working party. A complains to B about B's service to A. B advises the committee about whether A should be promoted. B consults A about new buildings for A's school. A asks for approval of his governors for something B advises against. B enquires from A about an allegation by a parent about his school. A serves on B's committee as a co-opted member.

The DES and the LEA are not in a direct hierarchical relationship : each has a function to perform within the Education Act and their relationship can only be properly understood in relation to that context. The same can be said of that between teacher and administrator : the authority and the role of each stems from the inherent legal and financial values of a given situation and not from any general dispensation.

This is only to be expected in a system which has evolved rather than been created. We have no detailed, immutable blue-print but rather an indication of lines along which development should take place. So it is just as important for education officers to be clear about future directions as about the proprieties of the present.

Evolving responsibility

Most administrators would agree with the move towards the acceptance of greater responsibility by teachers. This would have to include greater freedom in financial and staffing matters, for instance, and this might not be too easy to arrange within the traditional local government framework and the traditional democratic safeguards. But, since freedom is not synonymous with responsibility, it would involve more than this.

The kind of authority that could and should be exercised by teachers demands an acceptance of managerial responsibilities, sharing responsibility for discussions involving control and use of resources. Even within the present framework more could come into the discretion of heads if they, and their assistants, were more willing to accept responsibility and education authorities were less reluctant to offer it. Full professional control and responsibility will not come out of the blue, complete and entire. It will need to be made up of particular, smaller things : freedom in capitation schemes, staffing and allocation of above-scale allowances can pave the way to more spectacular responsibility.

The trend is already being set in the colleges of education and colleges of further education and there is no reason why it cannot come to the schools. When that time comes there will be more administrative staff in the institutions and fewer at headquarters. The education office will become a place for planning, research and broad policy direction rather than detailed administration.

It is time, too, that teachers had more influence on the curriculum. It is commonly stated that they control it, and compared with other countries this may be so, but there are serious limitations. First, individual freedom such as exists now is divisive and infinitely less powerful than collective professional influence could be. Second, individuals are more likely to conform to outside pressures than is a group. Third, the examination system has long dominated the curriculum. Fourth, the strong link between education and qualification for a job adds the pressure of employers and university entrance to the examination itself.

The Schools Council is giving a lead nationally in rethinking and reshaping the curriculum and provided it is acknowledged as a lead and not a potential source of prefabricated wisdom it will herald a big step forward. The nucleus of reform must be more local, involving every teacher in thinking out his or her own purposes. The groups must be small enough to stimulate rather than inhibit thought but big enough to carry weight. When this happens—and the CSE is a sign that it might—the profession can be truly responsible for what is taught in the schools. In view of the dominance of examinations reform of them is the most likely way in which the change is likely to come. Examinations, teacher-controlled and arising from the work of the schools, can precipitate change and liberate the curriculum more quickly than anything else. No one need fear that curriculum control by the teaching profession would mean an undemocratic intellectual bureaucracy. No three teachers have ever been known to agree fully on any academic question.

Partnership

The word partnership is a favourite in descriptions of the education service. For the most part it is a hope rather than a fact: some partners have bigger shares than others. But there has to be a partnership between teachers and local administrators if the service is to operate at all. If it is a good one this is our best hope of reconciling some of the antitheses with which this book began. Certainly some of the tensions between planning concepts, theoretical discoveries and pragmatic response can be resolved. But first we must look at the mechanics of partnership.

In discussing secondary reorganization it was suggested that the consultative processes needed in matters of conditions of service were different from those concerned with the actual reorganization and that the two were better kept separate. This applies to a whole range of issues on which administrators regularly consult teachers.

It is well known that education officers wishing to discuss a matter concerning secondary schools would if left to their own devices gather together a group of teachers from secondary schools: for primary they would choose primary teachers and so on. It is just as well known that the teachers' associations feel strongly that they should act on behalf of teachers whatever the issue. This makes sense: the teachers want to choose their own spokesmen, not have them chosen for them; and the administrator wants to speak to those with authority to speak for teachers. But it can be restrictive: the same people tend to appear, regardless of the topic, and they may or may not know much about it. Their thoughts tend to look first at the effect professionally of what is proposed, which may obscure the merits of the case. There tends to have to be a fixed number of representatives from each association at any meeting, restricting opportunity to vary the size and composition of the committee according to its function.

So it is helpful if issues affecting conditions of service can be dealt with separately: the pattern of joint consultative committees is then appropriate—agreed numbers of representatives, formal meetings at the request of 'either side' but with a main aim of reducing the feeling that there are two sides and of making conditions as good as possible for those who work in the service. Other matters may have quite different main aims—to discuss the introduction of commercial courses in secondary schools, let us say—and a different set-up is needed. In a matter of the second sort the main purpose is the discussion, and the frank expression of everyone's opinion is a necessary ingredient: this may not always be possible or helpful in the joint consultative framework.

The kind of instrument required is of an advisory kind, not strictly consultative. Many authorities have set up, formally or informally, something which may have a variety of names—or no name—but which we will describe here generically as a teachers' advisory committee.

This can be a large representative body which sub-divides itself into groups producing reports on various subjects at periodic intervals, or it can be a more flexible, less formalized affair. Whichever it is it will have to contend with the dilemma, in fixing representation, of the teachers' associations' functions. Conditions of service are not an issue and it is essential to bring in experts on particular questions. On the other hand to command full support any body of this kind needs the backing of the associations.

This may be easier to achieve in a looser, flexible structure. One way is to have a small steering committee to see to the mechanics and co-ordination of the enterprise : this is the body for the association representatives. The steering committee will then set up specific advisory committees, on topics suggested by the authority or the teachers, determine their membership, terms of reference and time limit. The advisory committees themselves can then be more broadly based, with members from all branches of the service and with power to co-opt.

Some topics will be specific and limited : such as the design of pupils' record cards; some may be broad and complex, requiring the production of long reports : for instance, religious education in schools. Within this pattern most of the *ad hoc* consulting that goes on can be fitted. It is a good framework for consultation on the design of buildings and furniture. New developments, such as local radio, can be investigated in an organized way. Recommendations can be put to education committee or teachers or both. It is a way in which the gap between planning and opportunism, theory and practice, can be narrowed. Above all it is a way in which teachers and officers can make their partnership a reality.

The teachers' advisory committee structure can include enquiries into curriculum development. It can help to co-ordinate and stimulate the efforts of local development teams who may be discussing, experimenting, working together, investigating lines of enquiry. Many of the uncertainties and imprecisions of individual investigations can be ironed out, and the sense of involvement, of co-operation in a worthwhile enterprise is likely to do more to stimulate change and improvement than any exhortations.

But it has limits, of time and of expertise. Enquiry can go so far but it reaches a point where organized research is needed to test its findings. Links between the teachers' advisory committee and the university departments of education and colleges of education can provide that research and perhaps solve other problems as well. One of the reasons why practitioners tend to be sceptical about research is the feeling that sometimes the subjects appear to have been chosen and the research undertaken for esoteric and unfathomable reasons, that it may seem occasionally to be an end in itself. One of the fruits of collaboration would be genuine subjects for research, of real value to the schools; its origins, the methods of approach and the findings would be better understood.

Of all the aspects of partnership between teachers and education officers, this kind of enterprise is likely to be most constructive and influential in the future. The administrator's contribution is two-fold: first in setting up the link and seeing that it works; second, in supporting by sensitive administrative and financial response the experiments and ideas for new approaches that emerge. And in these two functions we see the essence of his art and one of the many facets of his relationship with the teaching profession.

14

Education officers
and the community

Serving the community is not just an added attraction for the education officer to provide. It is not something to be grafted on to his work: it must permeate his whole approach. Experiments in community development are no use if the administrative basis of the service is not attuned to community needs.

Earlier chapters have indicated some of the requirements. The education officer has to identify and accept the democratic pattern of the service, considering the roles of all the participants in the light of the education acts. He must accept public accountability at every point, including being ready to explain his actions. He must seek a right relationship with all his other partners within education and work in conjunction with other services. He must identify the basic issues confronting his own service and advise on priorities.

The education officer cannot neglect the public's entitlement to an efficient service in his endeavours to sustain democracy. There is no room in his life for sentimental misconceptions equating informality and the personal touch with the haphazard neglect of administrative principles. He must seek to use organizing and planning ability to create a system that allows time for the personal at the points where the personal really counts. He must accept that he cannot do this alone, which reinforces the need for planned delegation of functions to his colleagues. The roots of effective community service are thus to be found, first in the education officer himself and secondly in the office organization within which he operates.

Conversely, a main objective must be to steer the system away from its natural preoccupation with the physical and tangible towards the people for whom the physical resources exist. Shortages of buildings and of teachers have tended to over-emphasize the importance of the quantitative in educational administration. To secure enough schools and to plan them well, to secure enough teachers and to try to attract them to the right schools—these are basic objectives and an education officer who achieved nothing else could hardly be accounted a failure. But not only are these objectives too limited in themselves, they can lead to neglect of qualitative aspects that are vital to education as a service for people.

It is natural to seek tangible expressions of one's skill, measures of one's performance that one can recognize oneself and that others can appreciate. They are less easy to achieve outside the quantitative, particularly if the pursuit of quality has to be through the democratic processes of committees on the one hand and team work on the other. Yet intangibles are the objectives that must be pursued if the end is to be truly community service.

They may be not only more difficult to identify but less glamorous than physical measures of performance. Accessibility to the public where it exists may be taken for granted; its importance is only clear when it is absent. The 'atmosphere' of an office may stubbornly resist attempts to give it an extra dimension of imagination. Attention to the style of letters emanating from the office may seem to yield only marginal profit in return for the effort it costs. Explaining decisions may involve an effort out of proportion to any immediate pay-off. Yet all three are basic prerequisites.

Much more attention has been given to public participation in educational affairs in recent years than formerly. A whole range of influences from the Plowden Report to such bodies as the Confederation for the Advancement of State Education, the Advisory Centre for Education and the Council for Educational Advance have been responsible for this. The Press and television have, rightly, given considerable publicity to criticisms of the somewhat exclusive attitude of education and to new ventures embodying the spirit of change. Some education authorities in pursuing new policies have perhaps neglected the less exciting but more fundamental job of first making what exists more accessible to public need. The patient, gradual revision of traditional provision is often an unrewarding task, but it must come high on the education officer's list.

Nor is it enough in breaking new ground to have merely a general objective. Involving the community simply for the sake of involvement is likely to achieve very little. What are the specific aims?

Involving the community

The concept of community participation in education has evoked some of the most enthusiastic and woolly-minded responses in the whole of recent social history. It would thus be possible to write at some length merely about what the various aspects of it mean, or could mean, or should mean. For example, the term 'community' is itself vague. Physically it can mean the street, the suburb, the town or even the conurbation in which you live. Philosophically it can relate to neighbours, citizenship, 'belonging' or a dozen other things. It is spoken of as a collection of people to be served, a social attitude, as a group with attitudes and aspirations of its own or as a physical entity. In the education officer's world all of these have their place, and the selection of meanings that will be discussed here and the order in which they are presented must be fairly arbitrary.

Perhaps the physical is the best starting point amongst so much that is impalpable. Educational facilities: schools, colleges, playgrounds, playing fields, swimming pools and so on—are only used for their main purpose on about 200 days in the year largely between the hours of nine a.m. and four p.m. These are resources paid for by the community and it seems both prudent and fair to make them available for public use provided they are not significantly hampered from doing their main job as a result of external use.

In the proviso there are problems which are objective and tangible enough but which may depend for their solution on the attitudes of the education officer. Shared use of a building by a school and say an evening class in cookery can lead to difficulties through dual use of equipment. Playing fields are not improved for coaching purposes if picnicking with its attendant risks of broken bottles is allowed; nor if they are worn-out by over-use. Playgrounds may be ideal places to attract children away from the streets in the evenings or in the holidays, but opening them up may affect the security of the school from vandalism. Local people in asking for the use of facilities may promise help with supervision: it may be inadequate or evaporate altogether.

These are real difficulties. In the end the education officer has to give priority to the needs of the children as pupils, and with a limited budget the economic advantages of multiple use may not be open to him. But the snags, and the lack of money, may be no more than a pretext for avoiding the complications. Giving priority to the children is not the same as putting the wishes of school teachers first, or aiming at a quiet life.

Attitude is again all-important in considering the next stage— planning future provision with community use in mind. This may involve sharing in the design of social and recreational projects, such as libraries and health centres: or planning new schools so that they can be more effectively put to use by the community, as evening institutes or youth clubs, including, for instance, easy access by handicapped people. There is imaginative effort required in the conception, the need to accept compromise in designing for many purposes within cost-limits, and the prospect of continued complications in the subsequent use.

Above all, however, the education officer has to contend with the prospect of some loss of sovereignty, since joint planning may, either actually or potentially, imply overall control of the conception by others. At this point we move from the purely physical to the notion that planning—town and country planning that is—implies more than control over land use. Today it more and more entails positive provision designed to improve the cultural and social well-being of the community. Again there is the possibility of a dilemma for the education officer and one in which he must try to be clear about his own motives. He has a duty to secure the best possible educational provision, which may mean that he must legitimately resist some of the compromises implicit in multi-purpose planning, but the resistance may sometimes be related to the possible threat to his own empire. Only a saint could be expected to remain entirely free from thoughts of this kind, and saintliness, if it ever occurred, would not perhaps be the quality most likely to produce the best administrators. It would be intolerable, however, if the desire for exclusiveness were to rob the education service of extra facilities that would not otherwise be possible than through co-operative ventures.

The education service has, of course, over the years pioneered many ventures in joint provision—the Cambridgeshire village colleges and the Cumberland projects are examples. The latest expression of the aspirations of many educators to fulfil the responsibilities given them by the 1944 Act in the spiritual, intellectual and recreational education of the nation is in the notion of the community school. The phrase is used to mean many things from shared use of amenities to bringing parents into the picture about what the school is doing.

In a paper presented to a UNESCO meeting of experts in 1964 Mr. J. O. J. Vanden Bossche of the Unesco Institute for Education, Hamburg, outlined some of the features of the community school:

> The purpose of the community school is to serve a community in a limited geographical area, a town, or a village. The community becomes, as it were, a laboratory for the school and helps the school by providing services or financial aid. The community school endeavours to improve living conditions in space and time : it offers its facilities to the community, it works out a curriculum adapted to the needs and potential of society. It is assisted by members of the community in working out its school policy. It promotes co-ordination of school and community activities for the greater benefit of all. . . .
>
> The curriculum, as mentioned must be based on the needs of the community. Its aim is to improve living conditions, concentrating on the most urgent needs. In a rural area, for example, it would be useful if the school could have an experimental plot where the pupils and members of the community could try out various experiments in cultivation, comparing the results of the different methods used. In areas stricken by epidemics the school will chiefly aim to improve conditions of hygiene in the community. Leisure time, which is a serious problem in many countries, could be put to constructive use in the school in the form of community activities.
>
> For this purpose the community school will put all its facilities at the disposal of the community. Members of the community can participate in physical and intellectual activities, of which they would otherwise have been deprived. The community school can also organize a baby-sitting service which would leave parents free to participate in cultural and sports activities. Not least the school will play an important part in preparing its pupils for their future professions. This preparation will aim at developing the attitude to work rather than providing technical training for a specific trade. In fact it is not unusual to find a person practising a completely different profession from the one he had originally chosen, or changing his occupation as a result of changes

in the economic structure. Thus the pupil must be prepared
to adapt to new ways of life.

Asuming that the community school has the support and
co-operation of the community, in what ways can the
community be of use to the school?

The community can help with the social activities, such as
baby-sitting, the organization of sports and leisure events,
and with travel and excursions. It could give advice and
occasionally specialists chosen from the community could hold
courses. An economist could give a talk on the economic
potential of the area, and the professional and labour market
prospects. A doctor could give lectures on hygiene. Some
committees could work on parent-pupil relationships and
parent-teacher relationships.

At its best the phrase 'community school' describes an attitude of
mind. For the education officer it should arise naturally out of the
whole spirit of the service he offers, and not be merely a rhetorical
flourish. Logically new ventures of this kind must come after the
transformation of existing schools and services. Ideally they will
arise naturally from what the people in the community want, not
what the planners think they ought to want.

Yet the education officer has at some point to refine and perhaps
narrow down his objectives as a servant of the community. Although
his potential field of operation is broad he is likely to be most effective if he avoids too general an approach—into say social service,
or recreation, or community development as a whole. In these he
is a contributor amongst many other agencies and his contribution
will do most good if it is shaped by and is closely linked with his
fundamental educational task.

Parents

Much of his concern in terms of the community is therefore with
parents. The enthusiasm and woolly-mindedness about community
participation generally applies equally to talk about parental involvement. There are two quite different aspects: one relates to the
articulate and intelligent—and generally better-off or at least
aspirant—parents' interest in the quality of education offered to
their children; the other is the growing awareness of the need,
largely unfulfilled, to interest inadequate parents in their children's
education and to help potentially interested but inarticulate parents
to play a more effective part.

Teachers may often feel threatened by the activities of such organizations as the Confederation for the Advancement of State Education. They can point to the narrow interests of parent-teacher associations (which have tended to centre on the arrangements for transfer to secondary schools). They can show that the parents whom the school really needs to see are often almost impossible to contact, and that a demanding few clamour for more attention than is merited. They value above all the independence they enjoy in curricular and organization matters and regard with horror the prospect of parental pressures and influence said to operate in parts of the United States. Nor should their fears be brushed aside : on educational as well as on professional grounds there is room for apprehension about indiscriminate enthusiasm for parental involvement.

Some of the anxiety could be resolved by clarifying what is intended by involving parents and in what way it should come about. One can feel sympathy for the idea that parents are at the end of the queue for consideration in matters affecting their children. But does this mean, for instance, that parents should be directly represented on governing bodies of schools? To ask how they would be chosen is also to question how representative they might be. The value of the representation would depend in any event on the effectiveness of the governing bodies and it is not unfair to suggest that there are worse features of the system of school governors than the absence of parents.

Parents may feel more justifiably aggrieved at their exclusion from matters that concern them vitally : for example, decisions about what subjects their children are to take. If the involvement of parents centred on matters like this then the apprehensions of teachers would be groundless : the parents would be involved *as parents* and wider co-operation could be expected to follow, arising naturally from their common interest with the teachers in the well-being of their children.

Even this kind of co-operation will not arise of its own accord, however, and the education officer must be prepared to ensure that schools consult parents on matters that affect them. He may need to intervene even more on the question of communication between schools and the homes of children in difficulty. This is because the normal machinery of the school is neither adequate nor appropriate for involvement in the delicate and complicated issues that arise when educational handicap is linked, as it so often is, with environmental or family problems.

So far as parents generally are concerned it seems reasonable to suggest that the main requirements are: that all matters of concern to parents should always be dealt with by schools, never ignored, though of course they may not be accepted; that schools should make special efforts to see that parents are involved, not just consulted, in things that specifically affect their own children; that the education service should acknowledge the need for and indeed make use of parental ginger-groups, however irritating or misguided they may seem to be.

Democratic involvement

The desire of parents to be represented on governing bodies is part of a general movement in favour of broadening the base of these bodies. In many areas there is a nucleus of councillors and the remainder tend to be chosen because of their political affiliations. The charge that this is undemocratic can hardly be sustained: councillors are elected directly by the people and can be removed by them and there seems nothing wrong in their nominating persons whom they consider suitable people to act as governors. What is more debatable is whether this narrow basis is the best for the schools: perhaps nomination by civic, industrial and other groups would bring about more significant involvement by different sectors of the community. It would, however, be difficult to organize a system like this.

More important is the function actually performed by governors and managers. The increasing and inevitable centralization of power in such matters as admission of pupils, repairs, provision of furniture, equipment and materials, and the traditional freedom of teachers to settle their own curricula, reinforced by growing professional strength, has tended to leave governors with little specific to do except appoint assistant teachers (and though this is an important exception it is insufficient to justify the elaborate machinery of setting up governing bodies and their administration). Their importance is normally said to reside in certain indefinable functions of a general kind. How satisfying and useful these are depends largely on how substantial they turn out to be in practice.

Traditionally the indefinable part of governing a school has to do with pressing the claims of individual schools against the generalized, unfeeling central authority. *Per capita* allowances, organized schemes of maintenance and quotas of teachers have long tended to diminish the significance of this role. Heads, too, are usually capable of pressing their own claims when there is any point in so doing. This emphasizes the diminution of another traditional role: protecting heads from the bureaucracy. Quite apart from the fact that heads themselves in many respects are part of the bureaucracy this has become much less necessary as the teaching profession has grown more powerful. In any event the implications of both these functions are in the end negative, and therefore likely to be unsatisfying.

Recognition of changing needs has led to recent proposals that the role of governors and managers should be redefined in terms of the community. They should it is suggested be a bridge between school and community and between authority and community. There is clearly much of value in the notion: it indicates a need and proposes a way of meeting it. It is, however, important to clarify what is meant if it is to be any more than a meaningless and ultimately frustrating slogan. How is the bridge to be formed? Teachers themselves are already involved in this bridge-building, along with many other social agencies, so that amateurism, however well-intentioned, is not likely to be either welcomed or effective. Perhaps for this reason specific suggestions are rarely made. Sometimes, when they are made they appear trivial—making tea at parents' meetings—or merely functional—running a baby-sitting service.

These ideas embody one important point—that bridge-building is more likely to be achieved by activity than mere membership of a largely impotent committee. Where they fall short perhaps is in setting the standard too low: even if these activities were likely to appeal to governors for any length of time what would be their long-term value? The emphasis might be better placed on the organizing potential of the governors. They would perform a real and lasting service if they were able to enlist and organize the services of local volunteers in the service of the schools, from parents' meetings and the consequent tea-making and baby-sitting functions to teams of voluntary counsellors supplementing the efforts of teachers, educational welfare officers and other professionals.

Developments like this can have wider implications. They demonstrate a way in which professionals and interested amateurs can co-operate to make the education service really sensitive to the needs of the community. They could be the first stage in reinterpreting the notion of voluntary service for the present day. Now that the old, philanthropic self-supporting voluntary agencies no longer flourish, but instead find themselves competing with statutory agencies, they are sadly in need of a new orientation. Equally society still needs their services, and the more complex statutory provision becomes the greater will be the likelihood of conflict between bureaucracy and people. At the level of the individual in difficulties there is often need for someone to stand alongside and help him to find his way through the complexities of the system : however sensitive the bureaucracy becomes it is not likely to avoid this entirely. And there is a need for leaders able to interpret the wishes of the community in relation to the long-term plans of the authorities. One of the education officer's tasks is to find effective ways of harnessing voluntary support.

The child

Voluntary effort has traditionally concerned itself with the underprivileged : its roots are in concern for the plight of the poor. Similarly, much state intervention began from the same concern. The education system began in this way, though it has long since assumed the role of a comprehensive service available to all who wish to use it.

And most education officers today have a special concern for the underprivileged. This is not because they think that children from more prosperous homes have no problems : they are not so naïve as to equate 'underprivileged' with 'poor'. If they make less positive efforts to help the children of middle-class parents it is because by and large these parents are articulate enough to be able to cope with the complexities of bureaucracy. Yet education authorities have not achieved success in helping the underprivileged commensurate with this concern.

In part this is because the analysis of the causes of educational handicap has fallen short of the desire to eliminate it, and therefore the remedies have been ineffective. Only recently have the many aspects of parental adequacy begun to be understood, together with the inter-relation of educational, emotional, physical and environmental problems. Only recently has attention turned away from 'secondary education for all' as the ultimate in ensuring equality of educational opportunity to the primary school years and even earlier as the time for intervention.

However great their concern and however good their provision of services very few education officers have been able to create administrative systems that even begin to be responsive to the needs of the inarticulate. That these needs are largely unspoken is one obvious explanation. Another is that the administrative processes do not readily lend themselves to change, and they are in their

o

nature geared to a certain standard of literacy, of responsibility, of respectability. Just as many intelligence tests require a certain standard of culture and therefore inaccurately measure what they seek to discover, so administrative machinery assumes certain standards in those it serves.

Some may think that excessive concern for inarticulate parents is out of place, breeding still greater fecklessness. It is arguable; but the real concern of education is with the child so the need is often to get beyond the parent. It is not enough, then, to accept, as some authorities do, parental satisfaction as a criterion in all cases. A new experiment in allocation to secondary schools was pronounced successful in a large and progressive authority a few years ago largely on the basis that fewer letters of complaint had been received from parents than before. Challenged, this was justified as democratic. Democracy is more than counting heads, however: the education authority, concerned first for the child, has to consider not just the surface of the problem but, for instance, the position of children whose parents do not know how to reply or who do not care enough about their children to take the trouble.

So whatever can be done, should be done, to make the service accessible to everyone. The atmosphere of the education office and its attitude to the public is important: the system in which those nearest the public—telephone operators, girls on enquiry desks and so on—are the least influential can perhaps be adjusted; what is needed is a positive emphasis on serving the public as a suitable part of the work of all officers, including the most senior. The office itself may be too readily assumed to be the natural place to deal with enquiries: the schools have already been mentioned, and there is a place too, for friendly, local places specially provided so that parents can call in when they wish and be sure of a welcome. Tea plays such an important part in the lives of the British, both dietetically and as a symbol of hospitality, that a small canteen or a place for do-it-yourself tea-making might repay the expense in a very short time.

But people are perhaps more important than places. Those who work in the schools and in the community—education welfare officers, psychologists, doctors, community wardens, youth leaders— might well play a more positive role in providing informal guidance services. Where teams of experts work in particular districts their own headquarters may make natural bases for meeting parents.

This positive approach to the inarticulate parent is, then, to serve the interests of the child. In refining the concept of the education officer's service to the community we must take the process further than the family to the child himself. Of course the service is for people of all ages but in terms of providing true equality of opportunity it becomes increasingly clear that it must emphasize much more than it has in the past those aspects that bear on the child in its formative years.

Thus nursery schools assume their true importance when they are seen not as part of a general service to the public, or even as a help to inadequate mothers, but as a way to meet real educational need for a child who might otherwise be so far behind by the time he even starts at the infant school that any prospect of equality of opportunity is already lost. So too the concepts of compensatory education and education priority areas developed by the Plowden Report; and the inter-professional guidance and welfare teams designed to detect at the earliest possible stage the many aspects of handicap. Concern for the next generation is the unifying thread that links the various ages and stages of the service. At the secondary stage the emphasis will be to secure teaching of a kind that will not only fit the child to work in the world and to live with his fellows, but also enable him to play a part in shaping the kind of future society he wants. And after school the system will provide not only through further education vocational and specialist training, but also in the youth and community service, opportunities for experiment in a wide range of leisure activities, and a chance to learn how the democratic processes work.

There should be no need to emphasize the importance of the child in the education officer's scheme of things. Yet the service has so many ramifications, so many interested parties, so many other features that may lay claim to first attention that children do not always come first. In the end the child is the education officer's client: it is by acting always in the best interests of the children that he serves the community best. And when he is able, in the middle of his preoccupation with estimates and committees, to take time off to visit a nearby infant school, he is doing more than renewing his contact with the classroom. He is reminding himself what his service is all about.

Index

Index